DARK

PSYCHOLOGY

SECRETS

*The Beginner's Guide to Learn Emotional
Manipulation Techniques, NLP, Brainwashing &
Mind Control. Discover the Art of Reading People &
Influence Human Behavior*

William Cooper

Table of Contents

Chapter 13: Toxic Relationships and Friendships, as well as how to avoid them

Chapter BONUS: 10 Strategies of Mass Manipulation by Media

1. The Strategy of Distraction

2. The Gradual Strategy

3. Create Problems and Offer Solutions

4. The Strategy of Deferring

5. Treat People Like Children

6. Taking Advantage of the Emotional Aspect

7. Keep the Public Ignorant

8. Making the Public Complacent

9. Reinforcing Self-Blame

10. Knowing People Better Than They Know Themselves

Conclusion

Introduction

Welcome to *"**Dark Psychology Secrets:** The Beginner's Guide to Learn Emotional Manipulation, NLP Secrets, Mind Control Techniques and Brainwashing. Discover the Art of Reading People and Influence Human Behavior"*.

In this book, you will find a trove of information based on the most current and up-to-date knowledge regarding psychology and manipulation techniques. If you are keen on learning more about this topic, then look no further. You have come to the right place.

When most folks think of the term "dark psychology," they often think of sorcery and witchcraft. However, dark psychology isn't about using magic spells and chants to control people's minds. That's hardly the objective of this book. This book intends to look at the tried and true aspects of human psychology which can be used to your benefit.

Hence, the utilization of psychology for your benefit is where the term "dark" comes into play. Since we are not looking to learn techniques that can help people recover from the trauma of other complex issues, this book takes on a "darker" tone.

In the following chapters, we'll be digging into the reasons manipulation, and mind control occur, how you can guard against it, and how you can use them for your benefit. Best of all, you will see how easy it can be to fall into traps that are set out there by manipulators.

Indeed, knowledge of the way dark psychology works will enable you to advance your agenda in such a way that you will be able to read people effectively while understanding what motivates them most of the time.

This volume is intended for anyone interested in learning more about this topic. There is no need to have an advanced psychology degree to understand these concepts. The effectiveness of these concepts lies in their simplicity. The use of dark psychology makes the adage, "the simplest answer is usually the right one" ring truer than ever. So, don't be surprised if the information that we will be discussing seems far simpler to understand than you had initially thought. Ultimately, it's up to you to decide how you want to approach this subject. If you want to learn more about it for instruction and enlightenment, then you will surely find critical insights that will help you see the world in a different light. If you are thinking about implementing these tactics for your own personal pursuits, then that's also perfectly valid.

The most important thing to keep in mind is that these are powerful tools. So, they should be treated as such. Therefore, do take them at face value, especially since only a privileged few really comprehend the way that they can be implemented to make their objectives come to fruition. As you read through this book, you may feel that the people who implement them are evil. Perhaps that might be true. But the truth is that they are people who want to get ahead regardless of the cost it represents to others.

Moreover, it's always important to keep a skeptical mind when thinking about how these tactics are implemented in daily life. There are several folks out there who appear to be one thing but secretly have a hidden agenda. These agendas hardly manifest in broad daylight but certainly, come to light when placed under closer scrutiny.

That's where this book will help you get the most out of your efforts. The more you are able to question everything you see around you, the easier it will be for you to get down to the core of why things are the way they seem. You will also begin to understand why certain people behave in a specific manner. Perhaps the most revealing part, certain people you thought were acting because they didn't know any better are doing it on purpose.

When reading this book, try to keep an open mind at all times. Some of the techniques that we will describe may seem somewhat outrageous, but the matter is that they work. This is why they are commonly used by advertisers, politicians, religious cults, and anyone looking to take advantage of unsuspecting victims. That is why we are keen on revealing how these tactics work in a digestible manner and are easy to follow.

So, what are you waiting for?

Let's get started with this topic. You are surely eager to get going with this discussion.

Chapter 1: Dark Psychology Secrets

When talking about dark psychology, it's quite common to think about techniques like brainwashing and manipulation. But the fact of the matter is we don't really know how deep dark psychology goes. After all, there is a definite method to the madness. We can't just accept that dark psychology is some random phenomenon that occurs as a result of people's wish to get their way.

The truth is that there is a precise method that can be applied in various ways.

That's why this chapter is devoted to analyzing the fundamentals of dark psychology and how it can become manifest in daily life. This will enable you to get a good foundation on this topic right from the beginning. It will allow you to begin to see the patterns that are evident in everyday life.

What is Dark Psychology?

For starters, it's worth taking the time to define psychology, and subsequently, dark psychology.

Generally speaking, Psychology is considered to be the study of human behavior and the functioning of the mind. However, broader definitions place psychology as the study of the mind and the soul. This broader interpretation makes it a bit harder to comprehend psychology as we don't really know what the soul is. As such, it's better to stick with the narrower vision of psychology which is the study of the mind.

The mind, or psyche, is a place where thoughts, ideas, and emotions can be located. This is important to note as understanding the fact that humans are made up of emotions will help you get a better feel for dark psychology. This assumption is based on the fact that emotions drive our actions and consequently influence the decisions we make. It is very rare to find individuals who maintain an objective view of life and the circumstances around them. As a result, most people tend to view things from their perspective as opposed to seeing things detached from their personal emotions and valuations.

Dark Psychology can be defined as the study of the human condition about a man's natural unconscious predisposition to prey on and subjugate others for personal gain.

This dark aspect of psychology is inherent within each of us, no one excluded, and is part of the most unconscious part of our mind.

If you plan to use psychology to help others manage their emotions and so on, then you are not in the domain of "dark" psychology. When you think about anything dark, you ought to keep your mind focused on the fact that we're talking about personal gain and benefit as opposed to helping others feel better about themselves. Now, it should be noted that we're not necessarily talking about harming others; it's just a question of using these techniques for your gain.

Dark Psychology vs. Covert Emotional Manipulation

When talking about persuasion, we're referring to the act of getting an individual to comply with a certain set of demands and requests as a result of a compelling set of reasons. This implies that the manipulator must find a way to convince their target so that they follow suit out of their own free will.

This type of approach implies that the target is acting out of their own free will. So, there is no manipulation to speak of. However, things change when we begin to talk about "dark psychology." In dark manipulation, we're venturing into a territory in which tricks and strategies are applied to force the target to do one thing or another.

Such tricks and techniques may include things like coercion. Coercion happens any time a manipulator looks to exert their influence through some sort of mechanism in which the victim has no choice but to comply lest they fact the circumstances of their non-compliance.

With emotional manipulation, the difference lies in the fact that the manipulator exploits certain emotional weaknesses that the victim cannot truly hide. For instance, a person who lacks affection may be tricked into doing the manipulator's bidding out of the hope of getting the affection they seek. Moreover, the term "covert" implies that the manipulation taking place is not exactly open and obvious. Rather, it is done in a concealed manner in which the manipulator's real intent is not evident, at least on the surface.

Now, it should be said that covert emotional manipulation may happen instinctively on the part of the manipulator; that is, the manipulator isn't fully aware that what they are doing is manipulation. This is common in people with narcissistic personalities. However, the situation gets dark when these attitudes are done consciously and with premeditation.

People Who Use Dark Psychology to Manipulate Others

This is a broad question to discuss as virtually anyone can use dark psychology at any given time. Perhaps the line can be drawn when a person stops using compelling arguments and reasoning to influence others and resorts to other tactics that might be considered inappropriate or simply frowned upon by society.

Such tactics aren't always sanctioned by society but are commonly used. That is why they fall under the "dark" realm because if an individual is caught using them, they will most likely suffer from some type of repercussion.

That being said, common areas in which you will find dark psychology are advertising, politics, religion, the workplace, relationships, family, and entertainment, to name a few. When you think of these areas, perhaps the thought of dark psychology doesn't immediately jump at you. But when you begin to peel back some of the layers, you will find that they are prevalent throughout our daily interactions.

Let's consider advertising for a moment

A common tactic, such as "limited time offer," is perfectly valid if the offer is indeed for a limited time. However, a long-running infomercial uses this call-to-action all the time. After a while, it's obvious that it's not a limited-time offer. It's just a ploy that's used to get others to buy right then and there. Perhaps a more forthcoming approach might have been, to be honest, that the offer stands "while supplies last."

The "limited time offer" tactic enters the realm of dark psychology the moment advertisers are lying to consumers. When consumers finally figure out it's just a ploy, the advert ceases to work. And just like this example, the world is littered with such ploys. The difference lies in that some are much more elaborate than others.

Another classic example is politics. Politicians spend a lot of resources trying to figure out what voters want to hear. Then, they go out and say the things that will resonate with voters. The same goes for religious cult leaders. They generally prey on the primal emotion of fear. They tell people that it's the end of the world. So, they need to get on board before they are left behind to suffer. This is how cult leaders gain a huge following in a brief period of time.

The Effects of Dark Psychology

The effects of dark psychology have a wide range. These can go from getting someone to buy one product to voting for a political candidate. It should be noted that we are not focusing entirely on mind control, which is the type of persuasion that can lead manipulators to order victims to kill people. We'll be discussing how each of the techniques involved can create a response in you that will compel you to get the latest phone or purchase a specific brand of clothing.

Moreover, these effects can essentially blind your sense to the real intentions of manipulators. In many ways, you will find that there is an attempt at your free will. Again, we're not talking about cartoonish attempts to control your mind. We're talking about playing with your feelings so that you can sign up for a cult or a political party.

In some of the darkest twists that you can find, manipulators find ways of taking over people's opinions and perspectives to the degree that a single organization can control an entire country. This can lead to the control of an entire social group by a reduced number of individuals. Of course, this isn't something that happens overnight. But when you are aware of how manipulation can be used, you will find that it's not quite as hard as it seems.

Dark Psychology Throughout History

There is nothing new about dark psychology and persuasion. These tactics have been around as long as humans have. Initially, persuasion played on the primal emotions of humans, such as fear, hunger, greed, and lust. Over time, these techniques, while still the same at their core, have become more and more refined. The result is a system of techniques that have become so subtle that the average individual can't figure out it's there; that is until they are clued in.

The persuasion was born in ancient Greece with the study of the art of rhetoric by the Sophist philosophers.

Persuasion has grown and altered over time since its beginnings. That isn't to say that the art and persuasive process haven't changed. Nonetheless, the art of persuasion and how it is employed now has evolved significantly.

Richard M. Perloff devoted a significant amount of time examining old beliefs, how they are applied, and how they might influence culture as a whole. "The Dynamics of Persuasion: Communication and Attitudes in the Twenty-First Century," he wrote. The book goes through five main ways that current values are being employed more than in the past. They are as follows: The quantity of influence messages has escalated to dangerously high levels: Persuasion was exclusively utilized in writing and in disputes amongst the elites in ancient Greece. There wasn't much convincing, and it wasn't something you'd see very frequently.

It is rare to travel anyplace in current times without some sort of persuasive message following you. Consider the many sorts and sources of advertisements available; in the United States, up to 3000 are found every day. Apart from that, strangers will come to your door, attempting to persuade you to buy something, believe in what they are selling, or try something new. Persuasion is more important than it has ever been in history in the modern world.

Persuasion is believed to spread quickly: in ancient Greece, it may take weeks or more to transmit a persuasive message from one location to another.

As a result, persuasion's effectiveness was restricted since most individuals were unable to comprehend the message. Many acts of persuasion have to be carried out in this manner, in the sense of face-to-face interaction. However, it wasn't until the early 20th century in which advertising, thanks to the emergence of the first mass media outlets, really began to take off. This new domain allowed folks such as Edward Bernays, known as the "father of public relations," to begin using covert tactics to get their message across to the general public.

Businesses have realized the power of persuasion and are doing everything they can to make it work for them. The more money they make, the more successful they are in persuading customers to buy their products.

Many organizations, such as public service organizations, marketing corporations, and advertising agencies, are exclusively concerned with the persuasive process.

With the rise of the internet, access to a global audience has never been easier. This is why social media has become so prevalent over the last ten years or so. We are literally in the midst of a revolution in which anyone with access to the internet can potentially get their message out there without much restriction.

We are not quite sure what the future holds. But one thing is certain, however people communicate in the future, there will be a way in which manipulators will be able to use those means to their advantage. Manipulators evolve with the times. So should you. That is why reading books such as these will allow you to gain insight into the mind of these individuals.

Chapter 2: Different Types of Manipulation Techniques

Dark Psychology is all about manipulation. As we have stated in various sections of this book, manipulation is meant to benefit the manipulator. So, when a manipulator sets out to execute one of their schemes, the intent is not to benefit the victim. The main intent is to find the means of exploiting the victim to achieve the manipulator's objectives.

Often, this requires the use of specific techniques, which, when used appropriately, can be very effective in achieving the aims and goals of the manipulator. Now, it should be said that some manipulators are quite good at instinctively carrying out these tactics. In other cases, manipulators may be well-trained in these types of techniques.

But one thing is for certain: if you want to become good at any of these tactics, you need to practice them regularly. Manipulation is like any other skill. It requires a good deal of practice and experience before you can become proficient at it.

With that in mind, we're going to devote one of the next chapters to the discussion of the most effective and thereby powerful manipulation tactics out there. Most importantly, you will be able to recognize them in action, thus giving you the chance to protect yourself against this type of manipulation.

Persuasion

Persuasion refers to the act of convincing someone to do something or act in a certain way. When thinking about persuasion, it should be noted that we are talking about voluntary action. This means that you are not openly coercing an individual to go along with your ideas. In fact, your ability to convince someone largely depends on the various factors that comprise effective persuasion.

On the whole, persuasion is about making a compelling argument that can resonate with others. If you have a weak argument, it may be nearly impossible to get others to go along with your ideas. By the same token, manipulators may rely on things like a charm and physical attraction to be persuasive.

For persuasion to work, your tactics need to somehow resonate with your target audience. For that to work, your message needs to reflect the values and beliefs of these folks.

So, your argument and reasoning could be so compelling that your logic would be undeniable.

A simple example may be a political candidate going into a town that's desperate for jobs to unveil a plan to create more employment opportunities. This would be a rather overt attempt at getting folks to vote for them. And while folks may be skeptical about the candidate's ability to create employment opportunities, they may feel compelled to vote for them out of desperation and hope.

Practitioners of dark psychology use persuasion effectively by playing on people's emotions. In some cases, they play on people's fears. Other times, they play on their greed. In general, persuasion can be quite effective when you play on negative emotions rather than positive ones. If you seek to motivate someone by telling them the benefits they will gain, you might be successful. However, you might be even more successful if you highlight what they stand to lose if they don't go along with you. That's why punishment is usually more effective than reward.

Manipulation

Persuasion, however, doesn't always work, even when you can trigger emotions. In such cases, you may have to take things up a notch. In this case, manipulation becomes the most immediate means at your disposal.

Before going into the explanation of the individual techniques of mental manipulation, we must understand the great mechanism that regulates our psyche because all the methods that influence human behavior derive directly or indirectly from this great existential rule.

All human beings are moved by two high opposing forces are "pain" and "pleasure." In other words, we can say that we are all neurologically programmed to "escape pain" or "achieve pleasure." Our brain is a mechanism that constantly carries out this process of evaluation between pleasure and pain.

Anthony Robbins, life coach, motivational trainer, and NLP expert, in his seminars he often says that "the secret to success is to learn to use pleasure and pain, instead of letting yourself be used by pleasure and pain. If you succeed, you will be in control of your life."

In the light of this very important existential mechanism, we can confirm with certainty that the levers that move people's behavior and that can, therefore, be activated to influence the behavior of others are related to three categories of emotions: pleasure, pain, and fear.

Depending on what levers I decide to use, I can try to produce a behavior.

To understand the difference between the various types of levers, we can take the same concept and formulate it in three ways several:

- *"If you buy this product, you will be satisfied."*

- *"If you don't buy this product, you'll be sick."*

- *"If you don't buy this product, there will be negative consequences."*

Each of these three levers can be operated by the manipulator to influence people, and this is done continuously, more or less consciously, by everyone.

A powerful emotion that you can trigger is fear. Any time fear is evoked in people; their primal survival instincts kick in. <u>This might compel people to go along with you simply because they fear the outcome if they don't</u>. While this may also be associated with coercion, the fact of the matter is that your ability to trigger these feelings will allow you to get ahead.

Manipulation can be as blatant as you would like it to be. You can be quite overt, that is, do very little to conceal your true intentions, or you can be much more subtle. The fact is that it depends on the situation you are in.

Consider this situation:
A supervisor knows that many of the workers in their department are desperate for jobs. They need their income and will do just about anything to keep their current job. Knowing this, the supervisor will coax them into working overtime regularly. Sure, they are paid for their overtime, but the truth is that they are being exploited. However, the workers will say very little because they need the job. And

even when they know they are being exploited, they have little choice but to go along until they can find another job.

Another good example of manipulation can be seen in relationships. One partner can manipulate the other by using statements such as, "no one else can love you as I do." This is a rather overt manipulation. As such, the victim, over time, will internalize the fact that there is no one else that will love them in the same way. This can lead to creating a type of dependency among partners, thereby limiting the will of the victim.

Neuro-linguistic Programming

Neuro-linguistic Programming, also known as NLP, is a widely used tool in various domains of psychological therapy and, well, neuro-associative conditioning. NLP largely consists of repeating phrases and words over and over again. The logic behind it is that if you can repeat something long enough, your brain will automatically pick up on it and pass it through to your subconscious. Once these ideas are implanted into your subconscious, they become a part of you.

That's both good and bad.

The "Neuro Associative Conditioning" is one of the most effective techniques designed by Anthony Robbins to get rid of limiting habits and behaviors.

In his seminars, he often says that "If you can't, then you must."

For starters, it's great if you are looking to cut back on negative habits such as smoking or overeating. It can provide you with the unconscious boost you may need. By the same token, it's great at helping your build up your self-confidence as these ideas are persistently in your mind.

However, NLP can also be used to plant seeds of ideas that you may not be aware of. The most common use of Neuro-linguistic Programming is in advertising. Companies and advertisers have slogans and jingles, which are used to position brands in the minds of consumers. Over time, certain words, sounds, music, and others are associated with a brand. It's a type of conditioning in which consumers keep these brands in mind all the time.

NLP can also be used to program people to act in a certain way. Think of the military. The military is filled with slogans and mantras that soldiers repeat over and over. The reason behind this is the programming of the soldier's mind. These mantras become so ingrained in their mindset that they end up tattooing them. It's part of fostering a sense of belonging. This wouldn't be possible, though, if there weren't some type of process by which these concepts were instilled in the mind of the soldier.

As for manipulators, NLP can be used quite simply. Skilled manipulators have a subtle way of telling people what they want them to believe over and over again. Such is the case of parents who tell their kids they are unable to do one thing or another. This is also the case of an individual who tells their spouse they are too fat or not good enough for them. This is also the case of the employer who constantly threatens their staff with firing them.

These messages, when repeated over and over again, eventually permeate the mind of the victim. If done long enough, these messages can completely overwhelm a person's psyche while leading them to feel destroyed and broken. For the victim, recovering from this type of abuse can be quite complicated and may take a very long time before they can restore balance.

Hypnosis

Hypnosis is commonly used in dark psychology and manipulation but in a very subtle and non-threatening manner. When you think about a hypnotherapist telling a patient "you're getting sleepy" while holding a pocket watch, what you're seeing is the hypnotherapist inducing a very calm state in which the target releases their guard. When this occurs, the target's subconscious emerges. At this point, any message can be implanted with very little resistance.

So, how can you achieve a deep state of relaxation in people without using your pocket watch?

A good solution is television. Studies have shown that brainwave activity tends to level off after a little as 30 minutes of watching television. At this point, brainwave activity resembles that of deep sleep. At this point, the individual is sleeping with their eyes open. Since brainwave activity has practically ceased, it is easy to implant ideas in the subconscious. Over time, these ideas stick, and you have individuals who are very responsive to your message.

Music is another form of hypnosis. A catchy tune can level off brainwave activity after a certain amount of time. This enables messages to seep through into the subconscious.

You can see this rather overtly in music videos. The tune helps establish a state of relaxation while the images get the message across.

Even praying is also a powerful form of inducing hypnosis. When a person uses prayer to connect with their spiritual beliefs, they are also implanting these ideas into their subconscious mind. In the end, they become attuned to the thoughts and feelings they wish to achieve. Meditation, for instance, is a great way in which a person can take ideas and make them their own.

Subliminal Messaging

Subliminal messaging is the act of encoding messages within a larger one. The most commonly used means of subliminal messaging is done through very brief images flashed across screens. This is the case with movies, television, and other visual media. Images are shown so quickly that the conscious mind doesn't register them. Yet, the subconscious mind does since it operates at a much faster speed. Since the subconscious mind picks it up, there is no need for the conscious mind to process the information. It just goes straight into storage and sits there.

The classic example of a subliminal message is the food commercials at the beginning of movies. These messages were incorporated by movie theaters to increase sales at their concession stands. Before the start of the movie, a song would play with images of food. However, very brief flashes of messages urging people to get up and purchase food and drinks were displayed. This experiment has been so successful that it is customary for people to purchase food and refreshments before the start of a film. This is where movie theaters make their money. The film is just the draw; the profits are made from the sales of refreshments.

Subliminal messaging is also widely used in music. Sounds, words, and other types of auditory messages are encoded in the music itself. Sometimes it's perceptible, and sometimes it's not. One of the most famous experiments of this nature is playing a record backward. This practice was done to uncover hidden messages in songs. While this has been proven to be purely coincidental, it does have some logic behind it. Since the subconscious mind operates at a much different level than the conscious mind, it can pick up very slight and subtle tidbits that the conscious mind may miss altogether.

It should be noted that the overarching intent of subliminal messaging is to access the subconscious minds of individuals. When this occurs, the manipulator can implant whatever message or information they want. As this message takes a foothold, people can be compelled to do practically anything the manipulator wishes to do.

Think about it this way:
If you drink a gallon of water with a couple of drops of poison, you may not necessarily taste the poison, and while it may be a tiny amount, it's still there. Over time, if you keep drinking drops and drops of poison, they will eventually cause a reaction in you.

The same happens with subliminal messages. These messages are hidden in visual advertising, movies, music, and slogans. You may not necessarily perceive it, but they're there. A good example of this is a catchy tune. So, the next time you find yourself humming a song that you can't get out of your head, you can be sure that you have just fallen for a subliminal message.

Chapter 3: The Dark Psychology Triad

This chapter will help understand what we mean by the dark triad, which is sometimes referred to as the 'the unholy trinity,' as well as what it consists of.

The Dark Triad is what ties up all other aspects of dark psychology. This simply outlines three personality traits that any person can have, which are destructive and harmful. The three traits that form the Dark Triad include Machiavellianism, psychopathy, and narcissism. Many will think that the three are rather too obvious, but each of them must be understood to understand what power they have.

What is Narcissism?

Narcissists are known to operate covertly, so they are difficult to detect. When the subject meets a narcissist for the first time, they might have thought that they were a pillar of the community with their lives beautifully put together. Perhaps, the subject wanted to keep this initial picture of excellence close, marking the beginning of their manipulation. The more admirable they are means that the more people want to give them shallow incentives to feed their hungry egos in their good graces. Thus, it is possible to completely go over your head some of the symptoms of narcissism. The misconception related to narcissists is that they are people that love themselves a little too much. In the realm of dark psychology, it is very far from reality itself. What are the distinctions between people with high self-esteem and narcissist? Narcissists have excessively high self-worth because their lives are different from others, for example. Not only are they unique, but they are also superior. Some of the signs that are seen in them include: they cannot accept criticism, and anyone who agrees with them finds it flattering. They need to be commended and given constant consent by people and to live in a manner that enables them to reach people who need to commend and flatter them.

Here are some of a narcissistic personality's most famous subtle signs. One of them is that they do not have a single bad shot. To find someone who isn't present in social media today is like finding a unicorn. It is almost impossible for people not to use at least 2 of them with the ease and exposure offered by social media platforms. Of course, this is an opportunity for your average everyday narcissist to shine on their reputation and improve their charade. Studies have shown that since the advent of social media, the commonalities of narcissistic behaviors have increased, suggesting that the two rising correlate. Social media basically acts as a platform on which a narcissist can move into his world. It is just like currency, and the more they have of it, the happier and satisfied they feel. That's why they aim to represent a version of them that is perfect on social networks, often even lying about some of the pictures to shift the meaning of the photos and create a better message. Scan the social media profile of a narcissist, and you will probably notice three things. They're not going to have bad pictures of themselves first. They will be particularly polished, with a lot of love and feedback, for each picture that contains them. Secondly, you can find that every day they often have perfect days. Every post deals with a beautiful family lunch, an intimate dinner, a bird chirping on their windows every morning. Whatever makes their lives look like they've been ripped out of a Hallmarks film. Third, they like 'smooth boasting' about some of their life's stuff.

Narcissists have a constant need to be right and battle tooth and nail to make sure they have the last word in any case, even when they speak to an expert. It may not be as pronounced at the beginning, but in small but clear cases, you may find signs of their resistance to correction.

A narcissist, in many cases, may seem right on every story, but they fight hard to get the final word. They will never come down and accept defeat, even if defeat means simply being right about the working hours of a restaurant.

A loud voice that demands to be heard is another trait of a narcissist. Have you ever tried to talk politely to a narcissist? They rarely take the form of a "chat." Speaking to a narcissist may seem to only listen to someone as you may not be allowed to tell your story. Narcissists believe that their only thoughts and opinions are theirs with an implicit sense of right and superiority. Any other results are inferior and incomplete, even if they are technically fine.

Obviously, this will not be understood by a narcissist because he will not even bring the light of day to other contributors. What you often find with a narcissist is that they tend to talk over others. They also take the opportunity of winning during casual conversations, giving others a few chances to interject. It allows the dialog to be driven in a way that benefits them. This is why you will find that a conversation with a narcissist is nothing more than a chat about himself on most occasions. Something is charming about a drug dealer; that's how they pull in their victims.

The exaggeration of the self-worth that narcissists undergo internally often influences their outward reality. Normally, the need for unity and applause and fear for criticism and dismissal are two ways to prove it. Loyalty and approval are like oxygen to the narcissistic ego, while criticism and doubt are like poison.

A narcissist has something charming, so they are reeling about their victims. Knowing that they need respect and praise from others, narcissists can draw insurrectionary victims into their supply of narcissism.

When the relationship progresses, they nourish their own narcissistic patterns, which are not completely blown but present in us all. We see that perfect person, and then we want to be close to them so that others can connect us with that ideal person.

It's like our teenage desire to make best friends with the well-known kid in school. The rationale is that if we are aligned with this perfect person, some of its ideal characteristics could rub us off.

Already, the narcissist knows what you want to do and will nurture your ability to be like them. They treat you like addition and ask you to do a fantastic job, to make you feel important, and to give praise to you that is rarely given to others. You feel dignified and confident, making you hungry for such praise.

Therefore, what you do is find ways to make the narcissist happy, do things to make them happy, and strive to hold on to the status. Eventually, you will find that most of your actions and choices are based on your desires.

When you begin to notice that your commitment is too high for someone else to endorse you, check yourself. If anything, you have to get your own approval. While it might be good to get it from others, it is much more important than any validation you get from external sources that you are able to accept yourself and be satisfied with your situation.

In summary, imagine a tyrant in an armed state knowing how narcissism feels. Such people seek reverence, build statues of them, and completely respect and honor those over whom they have authority. Any act of rebellion and disagreement shall be immediately and harshly punished.

Narcissistic Actions

One of the first indications of a narcissist is fantasies and imaginations of enormous strength and status. Many narcissists report infantile fantasies of adoration. While many individuals who are not narcissistic can sometimes dream about authority and status, a narcissist feels that they deserve this praise and elevation as the fundamental right. The fact that they are not always adored and venerated is an offense to a psychopath's psychological perspective. The conviction, "I'm better than most; they are not valuable to me," is a frequently held perception of serious narcissists. Most people experience self-image fluctuations due to their life achievements and conduct. It's not true of narcissists. Narcissists view flattery and praise as something they must receive automatically, irrespective of the changes they experience.

The inflation of the self-worth experienced internally by narcissists also has consequences for their exterior truth. Typically, this is demonstrated in two ways—the need for consensus and praise and the hate for critique or dismissal. Loyalty and consent for the narcissistic ego are like oxygen, whereas critique and disbelief are like poison.

Consider this situation in which two friends talk about going to lunch:

"Let's just go to that pizza place around the corner of East Avenue." "They open at 12 AM, and I'm always there for brunch."

"No, I'm pretty sure they open at 9 AM. They have a breakfast menu."

"They actually don't. It's more of an all-day breakfast menu. I visit them a lot. They open at 12 AM." "Let's just go, and I'll show you that they're open." The friends walk down to the restaurant and find it closed. The sign on the door says that operating hours start at 10 AM. Not wanting to look bad, the narcissist says, "Well, I walked by here yesterday, and they were open at around 9 AM. They must have different operating hours throughout the week." The sign on the door said that the 10 AM schedule was observed daily. However, the friend had no way of verifying whether the store was open at 9 AM the previous day since he wasn't in the area.

When you take a logical conclusion, imagine a dictator in an armed state to comprehend how narcissism looks like. These individuals request worship, constructing statues in their likeness, and full obedience and recognition from those they have authority over. Any act of disagreement or discord shall be punished quickly and brutally.

What is Machiavellianism?

A Machiavellian is someone cunning—unscrupulous, even. This trait gets its name from a man named Machiavelli, who was a philosopher. Machiavellians are people whose approach in life can be said to be very strategic. A Machiavellian studies the consequences or effects of a given action in terms of how it will affect the person carrying out a given action. They are good at taking actions that they know they will benefit from while trying to maintain a good image to the public. A good example of Machiavellian actions can be seen between former President George W. Bush and former President Barack Obama, where George Bush was considered a war president, and Barack Obama was considered to be peaceful. It can be said that they both had the same level of militant interest, but Obama was able to use this interest in a way that served his image to the public, which Bush was unable to do so.

Machiavellian Actions

We have stated that a Machiavellian is a person who is very much concerned with the image they portray to the public while they pursue their self-interest. It is very hard to recognize how Machiavellians behaves because they are masters of hiding their true intentions from the public. We highlight the well-known tactics of Machiavellians. Before we can continue, those who do not fall under the definition of Machiavellianism are people whose public image is a mirror of their genuine private life.

Machiavellians have a clear difference in how they come across people and who they really are. Examples illustrate this notion. There are many instances of serial murderers who have long escaped their offenses because their outward picture is so far apart from what individuals believe to be a murderer. An example is a religious leader who spends a lot of time working in doing charity and who seems to help regular people while committing horrific acts of violence and sexual assault when they are not doing charity work.

Another characteristic of Machiavellian individuals is the desire to exploit people. Think of a newcomer at an average office workplace to show this instance. If this person weren't clinically Machiavellian, they'd look around and see a space complete of distinct colleagues to get to understand. Every man is just like them. Some individuals are nice; some individuals are bad. A newcomer to the Machiavellian office would see each colleague, boss, or team member as a resource or piece of a puzzle to use and utilize. The Machiavellian person would see a sequence of strategic threats and weaknesses to handle, exploit or neutralize rather than seeing others as fellow human beings. This is a big component of why Machiavellians are so conscious of how they come across to people. They know this outward portrayal is the key to exerting influence and exploiting everybody they come across successfully.

When a Machiavellian breaks his pledge, he does so in a manner that makes them look noble and praiseworthy. An instance taken from modern politics can illustrate this. An instance taken from modern politics can illustrate this.

What Is Psychopathy?

When a random person is asked to define who a psychopath is, they will probably say it's a serial killer. The truth is far much deeper and scarier. The word itself is not really easy to define, but it can be said to be psychopathy, a condition of the mind that involves superficial charm and lack of human emotions such as remorse or empathy. We can say that a psychopath is someone who lacks empathy or remorse towards others. They are said to be the most dangerous people in the world, and they are like, as the famous saying goes, 'wolves in sheep clothing.' Psychopaths will come across as very charming and handsome strangers who immediately take your breath away. After this, they make it their purpose to end or destroy their victim's life. Many people have raised concerns about psychopaths' problems with society. They are able to get to the top in a field—be it in the financial sector or even in the criminal sector as serial killers— because they are not held back by human emotions in the decisions they make like most human beings would have.

Psychopathic Actions

Unless a person is equipped in the field of psychotherapy with access to a person, it is unlikely for the person to recognize them as a psychopath. Instead, recognizing the outward manifestations of psychopathy is essential because these are usually the only way to detect psychopathy before it is too late.

Charm is one of a psychopathic person's most prevalent external behaviors. However, it must be understood that this charm is superficial rather than profound, real charm. If you think of a truly charming individual from your lifetime, you will probably acknowledge that they have favorable character characteristics that underpin outward behavioral displays. It was a real expression of kindness and a willingness to make individuals happy if such a truly charming individual behaved charmingly. With a psychopath, this is not the case. Psychopaths can show all the outward indications of charm, such as physical appeal, obvious warmth, and interest in others. The internal motive behind these outdoor exhibits is why it is such a red flag. The use of this kind of charm is in order for them to have an advantage over their victims. With a psychopath, every step is calculated, and the charm is not genuine or deep.

Lying is another psychopathic trademark characteristic. It is not, on its own, sufficient to position an individual in the psychopathy diagnostic category.

However, it can show a psychopathic personality when coupled with other characteristics. Lying comes for a psychopath as naturally as breathing for most individuals who are psychologically healthy. Psychopaths do not show any outward signs of lying as they lack that emotional attachment or any related guilt. For them, lying was just something that they needed to do at the time.

Another characteristic that distinguishes psychopaths from non-psychopathic people is a lack of remorse. Many individuals who have committed atrocious acts, such as murder, feel a profound feeling of guilt and shame about what they have accomplished because of these emotions and even take their own lives. Psychopaths do not choose not to be remorseful—they are physically unable to do so, just like blind people who are unable to see.

Sadism

Sadism, due to the Marquis de Sade, is most commonly associated with barbaric sexual fetishes, but this idea is both misleading and horrible. We claim that one who desires violence is a real sadistic personality. Sadists find it enjoyable and thrilling to hurt innocent people —like killing— and, most specifically, they are looking to meet this demand for cruelty.

Chapter 4: The Best Techniques of Dark Psychology and Mind Manipulation

Reverse Psychology

A first tactic that a dark persuader can use is reverse psychology. This technique consists of assuming a behavior opposite to the desired one, with the expectation that this "prohibition" will arouse curiosity and therefore induce the person to do what is desired.

Some people are known to be like boomerangs because they refuse to go in the direction that they are sent to but take the opposite route. It works better when someone else is educated and chooses instinctively rather than thinking about things. They can introduce the intention to do X thing when they suggest the 'do not do X.' When you claim that you will do it, you may wonder whether you will do so.

A dark persuader can use this type of behavior because it is a weakness that the victim has. Take an example of a friend who loves to eat junk food at any opportunity he gets. The dark persuader knows this and therefore will suggest that they should eat healthy because it will be good for him, knowing that the friend will choose fast food, anyway.

Reverse Psychology can be used in sales techniques when dealing with a difficult customer.

The seller, in this case, can say: *"this is a product for rich people; I don't know if it can work for you because it costs a lot of money."* So the seller is like saying: "I don't want to sell it to you; it's not the right product for you because you can't afford it," just because reverse psychology leads the person to want the product even more.

Masking True Intentions (Door in the Face)

A dark persuader will also employ masking genuine motives to acquire what they desire. A dark persuader will conceal their genuine intentions from their victims and can employ a variety of tactics depending on their victims and the situation. People find it difficult to decline two requests in succession, therefore a dark persuader can try employing two requests in a row. Consider the following scenario: a manipulator demands $500 from their victim. The dark persuader will begin by outlining why $1000 is required and what would happen if they are unable to raise funds. The victim may feel guilty or compassionate, but they will politely explain to the manipulator that they are unable to lend the money since it is more than they can afford. This is when the persuader will reduce the sum to $500, which was their original request. They will associate the sum with an emotional cause that will make the victim impossible to decline the second request. The dark persuader makes off with the initial cash, leaving the victim befuddled as to what happened.

Foot in the Door

This tactic is implemented in increments. This begins with the manipulator asking for small favors. Every time the victim complies, the manipulator will ask for increasingly bigger favors until they get what they ultimately want, or they exhaust their victim. At that point, the manipulator needs to move on to a fresh victim.

Consider this example:

A manipulator wants a large sum of money. Yet, they know they won't get it if they just ask for it. So, they ask for a tiny sum. Then, they pay it back. Next, they ask for a bigger sum and then pay it back. They do this as they build up trust capital until one day; they get what they want, never to be heard from again.

This example clarifies why this technique is called putting your "foot in the door" and making room with your whole body...

A more rudimentary approach consists of asking multiple people for money with no intention of paying it back. Eventually, they exhaust the people around them. So, they need to move on and find new victims.

In the "foot in the door" technique, smaller requests are asked to gain compliance with larger requests, while the technique "door in the face" works in the opposite direction, where larger requests are asked, with the expectation that they will be rejected, to gain compliance for smaller requests.

The Blame Game

If the manipulator wants to make you do something against your will, he will have a better chance of getting that behavior by making you feel guilty. Blame is one of the most powerful manipulation techniques known to mankind. Guilt can be used to manipulate people by making them feel inferior to the help and support they have received, or it can also be used to make others feel inadequate for a "condition" they have. Think about all those times you hear people say, *"things would be different if I wasn't sick."* This is one of the most rudimentary ways to make someone feel guilty, but it is very powerful. Besides, you might hear others say things like, *"remember when you need my help? Now I need your help."* This is a clear attempt to convince someone to follow the manipulator's intentions.

Putting the Other Person Down

Through this technique, we try to make the other person feel less capable than he is. For example, you find every pretext to point out to the victim when he makes a mistake, and you do it repeatedly, to throw off his self-esteem. A person with low self-esteem is manageable and controllable, therefore manipulable. This way, the manipulator will feel in control of the situation.

When a person tries to manipulate you with this technique, remember that they will attack your identity, so they will tell you phrases like "you are incapable" instead, they will never tell you "you are behaving like an incapable person." To react to this technique, you have to detach yourself from this psycho-trap and think that instead, the person is judging your behavior at that moment and not your identity.

Leading Questions

This is where the dark persuader asks the victim questions that elicit a reaction. A persuader may ask something like, *"do you think that this person could be so mean?"* This question implies that the person will be bad in one way or another. An example of a non-leading question is, *"What do you think about that person?"* When we use leading questions, dark persuaders ensure that they use them carefully. Dark persuaders know that when the victim feels like they are being led in order to trigger a certain response from them, they will become more resistant to being persuaded. When the dark persuader gets a feeling that the victim has to be aware that he or she is being led, they will immediately change tactics and return to asking the leading questions only when the victim has come down.

Fatigue Inducement

The impact of mental fatigue on perceptual, emotional, and motivational factors is complex. Special effects, in the case of exhaustion, can be assumed to rely on the essence of the operation that causes fatigue. This study investigated the impact of exhaustion due to different activities based on working memory demands on brain function and efficiency. The results showed that driving quality was not impaired by exhaustion. The effects of fatigue on novelty therapy depended on the mental requirements for the task that caused fatigue.

Creating an Illusion

Create exaggeratedly high or unrealizable expectations, but present and sell them in such a powerful, persuasive, and tempting way for you that you'll end up believing it.

With this technique, it is possible to make the victim see the most beautiful future in such a way that she will be willing to do anything to make it happen, even spend a lot of money. The goal is to make people "daydream" to give them the hope of living their lives to the full.

Commitment and Congruity

Highly skilled and sophisticated manipulators know that building trust capital is essential, especially when seeking to build a long-term approach. Think about the most sophisticated conmen you can imagine. These are individuals who take time, often years, building up trust around them through congruent behavior so that others can fall into their trap.

At first, no one suspects the least bit in this individual as they have earned everyone's trust. As they gain more and more trust, they can use that trust capital to deceive others. This gives them some leeway in case they slip up. Given their track record, they will always have the benefit of the doubt.

This tactic is not common in less-sophisticated manipulators as it requires a great deal of dedication.

Impulsive individuals will never be able to pull this off as they focus more on short-term rather than long-term gain. Through this type of tactic, many manipulators are able to build a name for themselves in their chose domain. However, they are often exposed. When this occurs, the world is shocked to learn that who they thought was a pillar of their community was actually a manipulator.

One good example of this is a cheating spouse. An individual may cheat on their spouse for years without them noticing what's going on. Then, one day, the manipulator makes a mistake, whatever it is, and they are exposed. The shock that comes to the victim is overwhelming.

The reason why this tactic always backfires is due to the fact that the manipulator doesn't know when to stop. The longer they go without getting caught, the more they think the con will last forever. History has taught us that everyone gets caught eventually.

Reciprocity

This is the classic "*qui pro quo*," in other words, you scratch my back, I'll scratch yours. However, the victim doesn't know the extent to which they are being manipulated.

A great example of this can be found with informants.

When a manipulator wishes to extract information from someone, they may offer tidbits of information of their own in the hopes of motivating the victim to furnish the information the manipulator is looking for. However, the key to making this tactic work is that the manipulator must give information of little or no value while extracting information that may be profitable.

Manipulators also use this tactic when doing favors. They build up capital and then "call-in" favors. While this may seem like it's perfectly reasonable, it is a manipulation tactic as the manipulator doesn't do favors out of the goodness of their heart. They do it so that they can have people they can rely on in times of need. Alternatively, they can resort to guilt or even blackmail if the other party refuses to cooperate.

Scarcity and Demand

Often, manipulators realize that they have something, or at least have access to something that people really want.

When this occurs, they are able to manipulate those around them by creating a false illusion of scarcity.

Earlier, we talked about how advertisers generally use phrases such as "limited quantities available" or "while supplies last." These phrases have become so cliché that no one buys into them anymore.

Yet, manipulators can make this work by creating a sense that there is a scarcity of a product or service. Some of the more outright, devious ways of pulling this off are by planting fake informants who spread lies. When these lies spread, people may begin to panic and flock to get the products and services in question.

Another way of pulling this off is by spreading rumors on social media. Some people fall for it, and some don't. In the end, the goal is to create enough confusion so that no one is able to tell the difference.

Lastly, manufacturers may go as far as hoarding supplies in order to create an artificial scarcity. This has worked well throughout history. In fact, it's worked so well that it is illegal in most countries. Still, manufacturers can pull this off by controlling the entire supply chain of their products. So, any disruption along that line will cause scarcity, thereby creating panic in people. The manufacturers themselves are not responsible for the scarcity as they are not the ones who technically caused the issue.

Consensus

This tactic consists of setting situations in such a manner that people will agree to them regardless of what it is. Governments do this all the time. For instance, they know that no one will ever agree to a tax hike. Yet, they frame the situation in such a manner that if people wish to continue receiving government benefits, they need to accept the tax hike as there is no other way to fund it. So, people reluctantly accept the tax hike out of fear of losing their benefits.

A similar approach occurs during elections. This tactic is employed when voters go for the "least of the worst," that is, they realize that none of the candidates are good. But they'll vote for the candidate who isn't the worst.

In the end, this tactic is like "choosing your poison."

Bias

Bias refers to people's prejudices and presuppositions. People always have an opinion about one thing or another. So, the manipulators exploit this to their benefit. For example, political candidates run on a specific platform in their district because they know that that's what people want to hear.

On the other hand, you may find manipulators playing off people's fears. For example, a supervisor in a factory knows that people in that town are fearful of losing their jobs. As a result, the workers are reluctant to accept any changes that the company wants to make. This is especially important to the supervisor as they are afraid of losing their job. So, the supervisor uses the factory workers as pawns in their scheme.

Chapter 5: Covert Emotional Manipulation Techniques

Gaslighting

This technique has a bit of an unusual name, but its overall effectiveness is remarkable. Its effect lies in getting people to question their perception of reality. As such, gaslighting consists of manipulating the victim into believing what the manipulator wants them to believe, even when there is clear evidence against what the manipulator is saying.

It can be used, for example, in a discussion when one partner accuses the other of betraying it.

The "gaslighting" strategy is used to destabilize and make the other person doubt to make them believe that they are living in an imaginary reality. In these cases, one of the most used phrases is "It's all your imagination."

Another classic example of gaslighting can be seen in cases of abuse. The abuser repeatedly tells the victim that there is no such abuse happening, even when it's clear that the victim has been abused in some manner. This type of denial forces the victim to question their perception of the events that have taken place. When effective, the victim may not necessarily accept what the manipulator has said, but rather, will question their perception to the degree that they have no way of differentiating abuse from non-abuse situations.

Gaslighting is commonly used by politicians. This is why their first reaction is to deny everything when a scandal breaks. 9 times out of 10, politicians get away with initial denials. Unless the media decides to dig deeper and produce compelling evidence supporting claims, politicians will simply stonewall everything. This is intended to get voters to question the media's accuracy. The intent is not to convince the public, they have done no wrong; the intent is to generate enough confusion to where the public gives politicians the benefit of the doubt even when they are guilty.

Expert gaslighters are so charming and persuasive that they are generally given the benefit of the doubt. The fact of the matter is that this is all they need. So long as they are not indicated in the minds of others, they will feel content. To the degree in which the manipulator can sow the seed of doubt in the minds of others, they know they will always have the upper hand.

It should also be noted that there is a clear difference between simply denying facts and gaslighting. For gaslighting to be truly effective, there needs to be some credible explanation that can supplant the real events. This occurs when manipulators are able to come up with clever explanations for things that happen. That often entails playing the blame game or evading personal responsibility by concocting schemes. Then, there is always the possibility of creating a "boogeyman." A boogeyman is a fictional character that is created as a means of having something to pin the blame on. Now, the boogeyman does not need to be real. It doesn't even need to be a real person. The main function of the boogeyman is to have something which people can hate, fear, or blame for the things that happen around them. Expert manipulators can milk a boogeyman for a long time but will have to eventually move on to another one. In the end, it is nothing more than a fabrication.

The best antidote to gaslighting is to keep a close eye on details. Please don't forget that the devil is in the details. And so long as you can keep your eye on the details, you will be able to tell when you're being gaslit.

Emotional Blackmail

This is where the manipulator acts to generate empathy or guilt in the subject they are manipulating. These emotions are chosen because they are the two most powerful human emotions and are the most likely to steer others to do what the manipulator wants. The manipulator is able to exploit their subject, using their empathy or guilt, to compel others to comply or to help them achieve their ultimate goal.

Oftentimes, the manipulator can not only produce these feelings but can cause certain degrees of empathy or guilt, which are out of proportion to the situation. This means that they can take a situation—for example, bailing out at a party—to seem like one is missing out on a wedding or funeral.

Emotional blackmail is but one of the manipulators' techniques.

The Long Con

This is a slow method of persuasion. The long con is very useful because sometimes, people resist giving into persuasion because they feel like they are pressured or there isn't any trust between the victim and the persuader. Therefore, the long con will overcome the problem as mentioned. The dark persuader will invest their time in taking to understand their victim, befriending them, and ensuring that the victim develops a sense of trust and liking. In order to do this, the dark persuader builds an artificial rapport and uses another way to make the victim comfortable. After the victim has been prepared psychologically, the dark persuader begins at their attempts. They can start by trying to lead the victim into making choices that will be in the victim's best interest. The purpose of beginning like this is firstly to accustom the victim to being persuaded, and secondly, the mind of the victim associated the relationship between him and the dark persuader as a positive one and one that he will benefit from. Once the victim trusts the persuader, the victim is vulnerable to the persuader's actions and does not stand a chance. An example of how the long con is executed includes when, for example, an elderly lady loses her husband, she has been with over forty years. This elderly lady is befriended by a friend who could be a colleague who has the knowledge or even a member of a church. This person shows his understanding and becomes a rock to this elderly lady. Her guard suddenly drops when she is around this person. The person then begins with small positive acts of persuasion. The victim is thankful for these efforts and takes advice from the person because she trusts him or her. Being a dark persuader, he or she can persuade this lady into borrowing some money or giving property. Of course, this will not be the only thing he or she takes from this lady. If the elderly lady feels like it was just bad luck that happened to her, and she sincerely wants to help the person, then the dark persuader succeeded in the long con.

Insinuation

Another devious technique used to exert undetected mental influence is referred to as insinuation. The "innocent" manipulator allows what is a deliberately crafted, insinuating statement to elicit an awkward emotional response. If you take offense, he will inform you that it is not what he said. The comment is generally presented as a "compliment," but not very encouraging. But it's enough veiled to assume you underestimated. The trainer understands what will annoy you, and he or she will be happy to launch such a grenade and see how the fault lies. Their comments are intended to have various possible interpretations that will cause a lot of hurt and doubt. You may sound plummy or left without a meaningful response if you hear it at first because it has so many possible interpretations. As an example, your partner smiles and says, "What do you know? As a prostitute, you can make a lot of money!" If you question him, he'll tell you he intended it to be a joke. But you'll tell yourself what it means for a long time to come. You might ask why when your friend is with you speaking about prostitutes, how he first cares so much about prostitution, why he feels about you, and how much you ought to bring in the bill you're inclined to give. And you'll also wonder whether he would praise you, like he said, on how good a lover he feels you're. Such remarks will operate on you and intensify anger, potential disagreements, and partnership instability. It is convenient for the manipulator to make it appear like a mistake, but therein is the clue: the manipulator insists that he or she intended it just as an unintentional compliment. Of course, you did; typically, a compliment does not hurt your emotions nor makes you wonder what its true meaning is for years to come.

Insane Making

One of the other techniques that many manipulators have succeeded in is using a form of abuse called insane making. This technique is usually geared towards the idea that the subject is exploited to generate self-doubt; often, this self-doubt will become so intense that some subjects will begin to feel they're going insane. The manipulator often uses forms of passive aggression to create craziness. They could also choose verbally to support the subject but then offer nonverbal indications that reveal contradictory meanings. The manipulator also deliberately attempts to undermine other activities and practices while openly endorsing the same behavior. By any chance, when the manipulator is caught, they will use deception, rationalization, and denial to save themselves from drowning.

One of the biggest problems with emotional manipulators is that they are not always able to recognize the needs and lose the ability of others to satisfy or even take these needs into account. This is not an excuse for their actions, but often the interests of other people are not taken into account or are not a manipulator's concern so that they can exploit is not a priority for the manipulator, so they can conduct manipulative duties without feeling guilty or ashamed. This could make it hard to stop the action and rationally explain why the manipulator needs to stop.

Therefore, the handler may find it difficult for to develop positive and enduring friendships and relationships because those with who they are will always feel used and have trouble trusting the handler. This problem is a matter of established relationships; the manipulator cannot understand someone else's needs while the other person cannot establish the requisite emotional ties or confidence in the manipulator.

Love Bombing

Love bombing is a tactic that is usually used by emotional manipulators at their first encounter with their victims. This includes the severe, unexpected, and robust expression of positive feelings towards a victim. It may, at first, seem counterintuitive. Why do they behave so intensively optimistic at first if that person is trying to harm them? Because it suits its purposes—that's why!

This produces a deep sense of confidence, affection, and admiration from an individual victim to their manipulator, and this is the concept behind love bombing. Based on the analysis made by the manipulator, the degree to which love bombing is used and the individuals on whom it is used form the basis. A lonely, helpless victim who seeks help and consolation is likely to be more love-bombed by the manipulator because the manipulator will know the victim will be more receptive to it. Likewise, the more the victim is grounded, the less effort the manipulator will have to put into positivity.

The degree to which love bombing is used—and the person is used frequently—relies on the evaluation made by the manipulator of the scenario. By that, what do I imply? Take a person who looks very desperate, hopeless, and solitary, for example. The manipulator is more likely to choose this person as his recipient, as he is conscious that instead of his more satisfied friends, they are extremely receptive to him. From the above concept, two very significant items can be taught. You can see that we are exposed to two very significant classes on steady emotional manipulation.

The definition of the love-bombing technique offers two important lessons on Emotional Manipulation.

First of all, the hidden nature of Emotional Manipulation is well demonstrated. Imagine trying to understand that love bombing is a negative thing. "Well, this man was very sweet to me, and he made me feel very good." The red flags or warning signs of abuse are unlikely to be raised by such a statement. This is a textbook example of how something can be presented as something positive but has a negative result.

The second general lesson relevant to Emotional Manipulation that can be learned from love bombing is how emotional manipulation is molded in a way that fits into every unique situation.

Experienced manipulators have covertly tested and learned from many encounters in their history. Therefore, in any given situation, you know the intensity and timing of each Emotional Manipulation technique.

This is also regarded as a constructive enhancement—another strategy. Such a technique usually involves manipulating a person without it being understood. This is usually the stream of love bombing operations, closely preceded by constructive enhancement, after which positive reinforcement becomes eventually moderate. Why is that? Love bombing aims to lower the defenses of the target, which enhances their dependence on the individual who manipulates them. It produces a vision of intimacy or a positive relationship.

Positive Reinforcement

Intermittent positive reinforcement is a process that often chronologically intersects love bombing. It's a method to control a person without knowing what's going on. The typical series of the CEM situation of a textbook includes love bombing, constructive strengthening, and continuous negative strengthening. It is now apparent why this pattern is.

Love bombing is the unconditional, untrained, and severe show of the positivity of a manipulator in its early contact with them. It aims at softening the defenses of a victim, increasing their dependence on the person who manipulates them. It creates the framework for a positive relationship, friendship, or other forms of interaction.

The manipulator does not have an endless, unconditional positivity towards the viewer in this change of behavior. Instead, the manipulator rejects positivity until the person conducts a required behavior. For example, instance, the manipulator only shows a positive response if its victim calls it frequently. The client will not be aware of the strategic use of favorable feedback but will unconsciously fulfill the manipulator's desires that they are feeling nice.

Love Denial

You're not going to hear a manipulator agree to something false. Everything that has occurred will always be the responsibility of somebody else. We play the blame game very well. They're good. The refusal is, therefore, typically hand in hand with cheating. A manipulator also finds it necessary to fill his denial with lies about other people's actions.

Nevertheless, the manipulator needs his target to stay in place. We don't want to doubt their victims' acts and motives. If a survivor did, they could see other flaws in the marriage, and a manipulator would not want to see that occurring.

Reality Denial

This technique has an impact on the mind and not on the emotions of the victim in the first instance. However, the feelings of the said person will still be affected. One of the factors we dread as natural humans are that we must always think that we lose your winning health. If you believe it, it is a refreshing idea of missing your intelligence with an understandable account. How worse is that specific insanity, which is affected temporarily or permanently by a mental manipulator?

One could say that graduality is one of the primary principles justifying the rejection of truth. If a manipulator fires straight into the health of the person, the person is probably very badly wrong as this effort is detected. But more skilled manipulators know this and prefer to address this sensitive issue more carefully. Oftentimes, this is effective because manipulators are willing to erode one's health gradually until the decision they can no longer support. The erosion of the health of a victim undergoes a method that leads to its achievement. First of all, a victim has progressively begun to undermine his trust in his memories to a very mild extent. The manipulator achieves this by creating scenarios where a victim cannot be afraid to wonder whether it gives meaning to do what they do. The manipulator, if this is all planned, then will offer his own perspective of the subject, which is clearly the most trustworthy. This tiny erosion of trust is generally targeted at certain goals. The firms are usually to decrease the confidence of survivors in their capacity to comprehend this small stuff and recognize them. Instead, the other is to pass this confidence to the manipulator. The most important aspect that we should remember here is that the will of the victim is, generally, never the main aim of the manipulator, at first as he finds himself a little more powerful to remember. And like that, he has already demonstrated that the person can depend on somebody.

Triangulation

Another often-used technique of the controllers is that of triangulation. This is an effective tactic in a manipulator's arsenal, in which a partnership between you, him or her, and a third party becomes formed. The principal aim of this is to give the victim a feeling of confusion about the connection, causing the victim to have an intense love for the manipulator, that only makes her stay together for a long time thinking about the old lover she had, or simply bring up someone she always finds unexpectedly, in the case of gyms. It is much worse if you create vague, negative correlations between yourself and the other man. Their targets are concerned primarily about fear. When you confront them and inform them that your real problem is your depression and your low self-worth, they will lack involvement in the other man. Where were you listening to before? It is also no exception for the manipulator when using him strategically to view the other guy as his next target.

Graduality

Ever heard of those stories that someone was persuaded into taking their own life? Can this really even happen? It seems unbelievable, right? It can actually happen because dark persuasion isn't a bombshell or a sudden request. The dark persuader will take the victim one step at a time, just like a staircase. This doesn't sound like a big deal, but before the victim realizes it too late and there are almost at the bottom of the staircase. How does graduality look like? Take the example of people who commit crimes against other people. While thinking about it, take into account gang bosses or cult leaders. Such people will not begin by asking for the hard stuff first. It begins with petty crimes such as vandalizing property belonging to someone else or hiding things for them. Gradually the persuader asks for more and more severe demands while blackmailing the victim of the crimes committed. When the victim realizes his deep and has become easily persuaded into committing gruesome crimes because they feel like they have no other choice. Dark persuaders are very good at gradually increasing the severity of their persuasion.

The Law of State Transference

The "state" is a term relating to a person's general mood. An example of a strong congruent state is when a person's thoughts, words, and acts are aligned. The law of state transference encompasses the idea that the person with the balance of power in any particular situation can shift their emotional state to the individual with which they are communicating. When used by a dark persuader, this is a powerful concept.

If somebody tries to persuade people and understands the laws of state transference, a certain strategy may be used to manipulate their level of control over their target. At the start, the influencer pressures their state to suit the natural state of their subject. The influencer will force his state where the subject is feeling sad and talking slower than usual in the same format. Therefore, they establish a connection with their subject at a deep, subconscious level.

After a "state match" is done, the influencer begins changing their own state subtly to assess their victims' compliance. For example, the persuader can intensify his tone of voice slightly to see if their target is at the same pace as them. If the victim is showing signs of conformity, it clearly shows that the influencer has reached the hook point. Once a hook point is reached, the influencer is going to change the state of the subject to the state that they want. This could either be nice and positive or angry and negative, depending on the situation—it best suits the purposes of the influencer. This approach illustrates the effect of subconscious cues on the success or failure in the process of persuasion.

Mind Games

Mind games likely are the most overlooked and most significant elements in dark persuasion. Many people claim to play daily spirit games, but typically rarely. Like many people today complain that they are sad despite understanding what depression is, spirit games have the same destiny. Not every psychological activity is directed at an evil action. Of starters, while preparing a birthday surprise, the friends to which they rejoice must often play mind games in him to ensure that he doesn't think something. This is a beneficial choice because it does not affect the parties concerned. When you look at mind games from the point of view of sinister manipulation, your thoughts plunge towards the darker parts of our innermost desires. Experts from all over the world have taken a step further in debunking this trend. Providing some therapeutic method that usually focuses on the wellbeing of an individual and the power that a person has, it is the mind games that are the most harmful between dark psychological techniques. You do this for the sake of adrenaline, which has no hope for any particular result. Manipulators also fail to consider the victim's interests. A manipulator can continue to play sly games with his target, which encourages him to disguise his true nature and purpose by taking a cynical approach to his subject, which is usually the result of casualties because it is difficult to detect and very damaging to execute.

Chapter 6: Dark Seduction

Seduction and domination are such specific motives and behaviors that they are deserving of their chapter of dark psychology. Most of them have a relative seduced by someone who utilizes sinister behavioral concepts. You may have found some sort of underhand manipulation to your advantage in your activities in the world of dating.

The desire for the human sex is one of the most important desires, and the failure to achieve it can cause great tension, depression, and frustration. On the other side, some of the most well-known historical personalities have been documented to fulfill their sexual urges regularly and fully. The best girls in the world are often provided as a bonus for their high social status to Kings and Emperors.

King Henry, the 8th of England, is a particularly famous example of a mighty seducer. He created a new religious movement to encourage him to marry as many girls as he wanted. His attraction for women was so high. He even took full control of his spouses and ended up getting decapitated by many of them.

King Henry 8th is but one historical instance in the field of dark psychology of the position of seduction and lust. The existence and inspiration of this specific subject are a symbol of the fundamental aspect of dark psychology. A participant with an inadequate acknowledgment of the subject is unable to grasp how seduction and attraction apply to dark psychology.

So is all seduction grim psychological enticement? Actually, not so. Any seduction requires another person's search. This is achieved in a tentative and unstructured way by most people who do not know the abilities and darks of emotional manipulators. For this notion to be demonstrated, imagine the traditional romantic comedy scenario with a shy guy mistaking his girl's chase. In

Madness, stumbled romance or Will Smith in Hitch is like a skillful mental seducer.

The use of dark psychology as a way of persuading people, as you see in this section, is neither good nor bad necessarily. The effect on the seduced man can only measure this. A whole part of this chapter is about the distinction between moral and immoral seduction.

And how can we use this chapter? At least, the comprehension of Dark Psychology as a general concept will be finished. Any book that does not include seduction specifics would be incomplete. You can also practically use the data you want. It is entirely your choice whether you choose to shield yourself or your loved ones from the dark seducers. Every segment will alter your perspective on dating for the rest of your life.

Why Cognitive Darkness?

One of the important questions as people learn about dark emotional seduction for the first time is, "Why?" Why does this one-of-a-kind allure draw people? Isn't it easier to go to court on dates in a more gradual and open manner? Understanding why people choose the route of dark seduction is the first step toward appreciating their great power.

Consider someone who goes about their love life without employing any of the dark psychology universe's advice or practices. A "conventional dater" is someone who spends a lot of time and money on someone before they have sex. You can divorce them and still make a public pledge of loyalty and dedication.

The typical dater, who is now a conventional wife, may discover that their lives are not going as planned. They entered the marriage with high expectations, but their husbands failed to deliver. For both parties, there is a choice. In a barren or unhappy relationship, they live and cheat on their partner. Who would desire a path?

Such deceptive current evidence is coupled with the happy seducer who uses dark psychology to obtain whatever he or she wants out of the domain of love. No one else is too critical, and they learn how to utilize dark manipulation to locate someone else, resulting in a carefree, reckless attitude toward life.

If a seducer is eager to settle down, he does it without feeling like he's "settling down" and plunging into his first marriage. In truth, because it arises from abundance rather than scarcity, this leads to a healthier, happier relationship.

How can a seducer who is content in the dating world gain such reputation and clout? It is related to our ability to apply strategies that are derived from the concepts we understand. Throughout the narrative, we've seen several illustrations of how dark psychology works in various sectors of existence. What's the difference between dating and seduction?

Dark psychology has a near-secret weapon grasp of the human psyche, which is one of their primary advantages over the competition. If conventional information is a tortured person who unintentionally stumbles across the love cosmos and listens to what happens, the professional seducer is a stalker, stalking and doing whatever he wants.

Anyone looking for dark cognitive theories in the server world is likely to be surprised by the disparity between their encounters and past efforts. A history of uncertainty, sorrow, and vulnerability is replaced by a sense of control and assurance. Surprisingly, the dark therapist will realize that not only does he or she feel much better about his or her own performance, but that the people with whom he or she speaks often enjoy the experience considerably more as well. This is because dark psychology informs a seducer about what others in the dating scene seek and pushes the seducer to pursue it.

Many who have, for the first time, used their dark intuitive abilities to describe the world of meditation and seduction as a moment of eureka. You will acquire what you want out of life by fulfilling your deepest, longest-lasting wish using these approaches and concepts.

Is Dark Seduction a Bad Thing?

One of the newest concerns about the theory of dark emotional seduction is whether methods are, in some sense, unethical or bad. Deep emotional seduction isn't good or bad, like almost nothing. How it is used determines how objectively it is judged. With one of three simple motivations, people use dark emotional seductions–to help people, they seduce, harm, and support themselves only.

It is hard for many to accept that anyone will enter the world of dark mental seduction to help anyone. Obviously, any seducer is greedy and carefree, right? Right. False.

One of the world's best-recognized theories about seduction is "find them happier than they have been discovered." People who hold this opinion do not believe that someone has to "loses" in the cycle of seduction. All sides—the seducer and the seduced man—can have a "gain/gain" encounter in which nobody loses.

So how does a person profit from a seductive lifestyle when they are more comfortable than they have found? The principle behind moral seduction is never to cheat or deceive the target outright. The universe is expected and offering nothing, one of the most common features for insincere men. Fellow seducers make no promises that they are unable to satisfy.

Instead, they simply allow the seducing individual to enjoy the experience in its entirety.

Many people join with less pure motives into the realm of deep mental ruin. They only need to fulfill their own needs and desires, and they are happy to lead the person they seduce, injure, or harm. This reckless narcissism is paradoxically enticing to some who bizarrely come back to habits that are frequently used.

Someone's conduct that does not matter for others without their own gratification also leads to problems with their emotional seduction. Without a truly carefree, rebellious attitude, people go into a realm of seduction, and difficulties emerge. This kind of seducer also contributes to unwanted children and a lot of support for children getting compensated. They are more apt to evoke the rage of their disregarded conquests. Those with too much cavalry have been killed and wounded by former lovers in their enticement.

Two essential solutions have now been addressed to the sinister emotional seduction of others and those who want to harm others. We are now going to look at the third way—the adult who only cares about his own life.

Somebody who uses Dark Psychological Seduction as a strategy that applies primarily to his existence and effects will most certainly treat the seductive method as "self-development of a drug" and instead push the boundaries of what is possible in the world of socializing, pressure people to discover their abilities and then Then, use a methodology that is only important for their lives and to their performance.

Such people are more likely to profit from testing and shaping societal rules and conventions than from the traditional solution they obtain. Such a route is close to the one that someone takes with a focused effort and self-amelioration from overweight to safe. You have less effect on the men you seduce than on themselves. A dark seduction has less impact on them.

Chapter 7: Neuro-Linguistic Programming for Influence

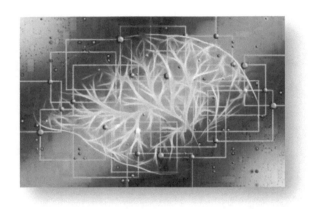

What is Neuro-Linguistic Programming?

NLP is a technique that involves psychological techniques where there is communication with the victim's subconscious or unconscious mind. If we can break down the word, we would have neuro to mean nerves (act as a way of communication by the brain), linguistic to mean language, and lastly, programming, which here means how something works.

NLP can be used by a person to enhance their intelligence, how they communicate with others, their mindset, and even their appearance should they want to. NLP has the power to modify or change any part of one's self or even others. NLP is a very powerful tool when used in the right manner.

NLP Modelling

The method of reconstitution and duplication of perfection is NLP Modeling. Set it up in individuals, groups, and organizations. We may design all human behavior by understanding the principles, the psychology, and the basic mechanisms of reasoning (that's the strategy) that are the foundation of capacity and behavior. The measure for effective modeling is–teach them why. Can they do that?

A Brief History of NLP

NLP began in the 1970s and is associated with Richard Bandler, who was a student studying mathematics and computer science. He later majored in behavioral science, and this is where NLP came to be. Richard Bandler teamed up with Dr. John Grinder. Dr. John Grinder was a linguistics professor, and from this, NLP began through computer programming and linguistics.

Core Concepts of NLP

NLP's core philosophy is built on three essential pillars. From these pillars, other researchers and practitioners have expanded upon them. So long as these three pillars are respected, NLP is believed to work and be effective. To reach their maximum potential, practitioners need to pay close attention to the way these pillars interact with one another.

Subjectivity

The first pillar, or core concept, is subjectivity. This concept is based on the fact that we all have different perceptions of the world around us. And while there are universal concepts that are believed and accepted, the fact of the matter is that we all have experience which differs to a varying degree.

Moreover, subjectivity is the basis of human experience. Therefore, we need to engage all of our senses to perceive the world as best we can. This is why educators who implement NLP seek to engage all five senses within the learning experience. That way, learners can get a good sense of the content they are trying to internalize.

Consciousness

NLP is predicated on the fact that the human psyche is built on a dual-layer of consciousness and unconsciousness. In this manner, the human psyche uses consciousness to express rationality for the things that we do on a daily basis. On the flip side, unconsciousness is the instinctive manifestation of the built-in programming that we have accrued over the course of our evolution.

Learning

Learning takes place when the conscious internalization of the world around us is achieved through the perception that is generated by the senses. When a person can internalize content or their particular perception of the experiences they live, they can transform this into learning. This is why experience is crucial to the effectiveness of NLP. Unless a human is unable to experience the world, meaningful learning cannot fully take place.

Albert Mehrabian

He was interested in the study of the importance of non-verbal cues and how sometimes it conflicts with face-to-face conversations. He came up with a model that consisted of three basic elements: face-to-face communication of emotions, non-verbal communication (gestures, body language, intonation), and lastly the spoken word.

The result was shocking:

- The words, the verbal content, count for only 7%;

- Para-verbal communication (tone, volume, voice rhythm, etc.) accounts for 38%;

- Non-verbal communication (especially body and facial mimicry) influences 55%.

Communication Verbal and Para-Verbal

Verbal communication is often misrepresented as words and language. And while that is the core component of verbal communication, the fact of the matter is that words, in themselves, are meaningless when faced with other components such as tone of voice, pitch, speed, and volume. For most individuals, picking up on these contextual clues is instinctive; that is, they are trained to recognize them from an early age. However, they don't rationalize what they mean.

Therefore, verbal communication is an essential factor when it comes to getting a message across (count for only 7%). Even the most hateful comment can seem less damaging if it is delivered in a friendly tone. The most beautiful words can be delivered in a somber tone, thereby ruining their intended effect (influences 38%).

The fact of the matter is that verbal communication is tailored to suit the need of the manipulator. In some contexts, manipulators may be dismissed as hypocritical and false. Yet, they know when to smile and sound cheerful, especially when that means extracting some type of gain from their counterparts. A good example of this can be seen in salesmen. They automatically turn on the charm when they want to woo a customer. Once they have made the sale, they can revert to their real selves.

As such, skilled manipulators know how to use their voice and when to play with it. They will find the best way to get their message across while making sure that they implant their true intentions. That way, the individual will react in the manner they seek.

Non-Verbal Communication

Non-verbal communication makes up the bulk of human communication. It is said that 55% of communication is non-verbal. This means that the way we dress, act, and gesture all point toward our true intentions. This means that you can betray your words by acting in a manner that contradicts what you are trying to portray outwardly.

This is why manipulators pay close attention to their gestures, body language, and mannerisms. They know that if they do one thing or fail to do the other, they run the risk of blowing their cover. One of the most common things that manipulators do is have some type of prop with them. This could include a cigarette, a cup of coffee, a phone, or anything they can use to diffuse any unconscious mannerism. Able manipulators are adept at smiling when they have to and feigning sadness when they have to. They are keenly aware of the way they are expected to act in a given situation and will do so, especially when they don't feel in that particular manner.

Rapport NLP

Rapport is very important in everyday relationships with other people. Rapport is that connection you get with someone, and it's like, "We are going to be such good friends."

A lot happens when we see a friendly face or a smile. The brain processes the picture in a manner that it can understand. This picture created is sent to the thalamus. The thalamus then takes the picture and sends it to the frontal lobes, where we become aware. At the same time, facial muscles are used to show happiness or pleasure. The information then travels back to the thalamus, which is then stored in the limbic system. The limbic system has the task of using this information and translating it into the form of emotions and happiness. The body (amygdala) creates the emotion of pleasure where we are able to feel other people's feelings.

Mirroring and Matching

Breathing Pattern

Usually, when people speak, they breathe out. Combine this behavior when the person talks. You take a similar breath when the individual breathes in. When you chat, talk, and breathe out when the man breathes in. Inhale the oxygen at the same moment. You can understand and predict the breathing pattern by looking at the top of your shoulders. The shoulder rise will show an inhalation, while the shoulder drop will show an expiration.

Posture and Gesture

Many people use movements and expressions to explain the way their perceptions are categorized. Observe each, in a sense, gracefully time and balance emotions. Does your client communicate with their hands or by tilting and nodding their heads? Are hand movements repetitive, broad, defensive, or restrictive? Reflect the movements of the person you are talking to discreetly—just wait a few seconds and lean to the right as they move their head towards the ground.

Body Orientation

Communication also represents perceptions and emotions. You begin to understand more about him when you mimic and suit the body posture of someone. Does your customer sit, walk, rest, and slouch? Were her arms crossed and her legs? Should she lean in a specific direction? Are her feet different or together? Will she have anything like a coffee pen or cup? When you cross your legs and put your hands on a plate, pause 4-5 seconds and make the same move.

Energy

This means that the manager is completely focused on the issue and deliberately ignores any of its concerns.

Verbal Language

Verbal communication is both written and spoken in words. Oral interaction generally refers to the use of speech. In contrast, nonverbal contact relates to communication through ways other than speaking—for instance, body language, movements, and silence.

Volume, Tone, Speed, and Speech

The consistency of the voice, the sound, the size, pace, etc., are important elements of interaction. It's a great way to build friendships to suit the voice of someone. Try to match as much of your speech as possible, but don't try to demonstrate your imitation abilities. If a soft voice occurs, the language must suit the softness. If a person speaks fast, try talking at a similar pace without gibberish speech. You speak loudly without upsetting the neighbors, too, if a person speaks loudly. According to neuronal language training, it is easier to mimic, fit, or mirror by adapting somebody's speech with you immediately.

Chunk Size in Their Language

Chunking is a term that refers to the process of collecting and grouping individual data elements (chunks) into larger pieces. By bringing every object together, the amount of information you remember can be improved.

Anchoring in NLP

Types

NLP Anchoring is a good way to discuss the first type of NLP. A great way to think about how to guide an album that you are acquainted with. Have you ever been sitting in a car listening to a track you didn't hear in a long time? Has this album caused a kind of feeling from the past in you? The first time you heard this song or sometimes when you heard it, you went through these sensations, and this particular song was attached to your unconscious mind. The song would become an anchor of these sentiments through this process. Now, any time you hear this particular song, you cause the brain to enjoy it again. This is a great anchoring illustration.

Designs

Most hypnotists find that anchoring is a beneficial tool for their participants to be hypnotized. For example, when you recall getting punished for doing something good in the past, the hypnotist can get into a particular memory and allow you to replicate the emotions you felt. At the same time, during your recreation, the hypnotizer will have you take some sort of action to touch your fingers together.

Installation

Now, you can have the same happy feelings again each time you touch your fingertips together. The anchoring process can work to motivate you to achieve something with good feelings. This approach is often used to help people find the strength to commit to weight loss and a diet. The hypnotist deals with the subject to create a positive focus connected to the subject's mental image—in this case, the subject thinks of itself in a slim sexy body. If the object re-images this picture, it stimulates the anchor and gets the optimistic push that it wants. The desire for weight loss in hypnosis is significantly dramatically increased compared with those who do not. In various instances, the anchoring process can be used to help the person improve himself.

Tips

You must be confident enough to know when someone experiences the feelings you want to evoke to use the anchoring of your sensory acuity. As the sensation rises to the top, you "fix" the anchor in order to bring in the atmosphere that you want to connect to. Consider how, in a romantic setting, anchoring takes place. A relationship is built up, and as you look at the person, hot and fuzzy emotions begin to grow. This alone puts the emotions into touch with the subject so that you only have to think and feel the face of the person. But you can use this to speed up these feelings by deliberately using the anchoring mechanism.

"Pleasure" and "Pain": Two Powerful Leverage

We have already said that our brain systematically leads us to make choices that avoid pain and possibly lead us to pleasure. But some are more sensitive to the "pain leverage" and those who are more sensitive to the "pleasure leverage."

People "Towards Pleasure"

People drove more by "pleasure" are called in neuro-linguistic programming the "towards pleasure," in the sense that they go towards things, they are focused on what they want to happen, they are open to change.

For example, there are people to whom if (using the pleasure leverage) you say: *"Come to the sea, and we'll have fun and stay cool,"* they don't move at all, but they are sensitive to the pain leverage and so if we say: *"Come to the sea with us instead of staying at home to get bored and suffer the heat."* They'll accept, and they'll start.

People "towards pleasure" often ask themselves, "what is there to gain?" and are focused on the positive emotions they will feel when they reach the final result.

If you know people "towards pleasure" and you want to persuade them, it is better that you tell them about the "pleasures" or the advantages they will get if they do what you propose. These people are activated when there is something to conquer. They're motivated by the awards.

Here are some examples:

"If you want to make money, then you have to listen to me."

"If you want to win, then you have to do what I say."

"If you want to be the best, then you have to follow these directions."

People "Away From Pain"
People motivated by the leverage "pain" instead are called "away from pain" because they are focused on avoiding problems, running away from everything painful or annoying.

People "away from pain," ask themselves, "what is the risk in this thing?" they prefer to think about the problem and how to avoid it; they tend to see the flaws in things.

If you have to persuade a "way out of pain," it is better that you describe to him the "pains" or the problems, the possible negative consequences that he might face if he does not do what you propose. These people are activated when there is a problem to be solved. They're motivated by threats.

Here are some examples:

"If you want to avoid a big problem, then you have to listen to me."

"If you want to be quiet, then you have to do what I tell you."

"If you don't want to make a mistake, then you must follow these directions."

Chapter 8: The Power of Persuasion

We have discussed persuasion throughout this book. In this discussion, we have underlined the fact that persuasion is all about creating a compelling reason for a person to go along with the manipulator's will and desires. In many cases, persuasion has nothing dark about it. Other times, there may have to be a little more work put in so that others can be compelled to follow suit.

In general, persuasion is about creating a set of conditions in which individuals can find no reason to go against what is being asked of them. In this manner, the conditions are created to enable the manipulator to find the right means of getting through to people.

Consider the case of rapport:

Previously, we mentioned how rapport essentially functions as a means of getting others to like and get along with you. But rapport isn't something that just happens on its own. Rapport requires a good deal of skill for it to be effective. As such, the manipulator needs to create a set of conditions that are conducive to rapport. For example, if you're going into a sales meeting, you want to make sure that your potential customers are relaxed and feeling confident. If they are uncomfortable in any way, that can end up sabotaging your plans to make the most of your opportunity.

That is why persuasion is partly a question of your personal skills and the situation that you find yourself in. You can have the most compelling argument in the world. But if you don't build the right conditions around you, then the chances of you making headway will be slim. On the contrary, even a weak argument can make a good impact if the conditions are right.

The Six Principles of Persuasion by Dr. Robert Cialdini

Persuasion is governed by six major principles. These principles are what provide the foundational reasoning for persuasion to be effective. So, when considering the effects of persuasion, it's important to make sure that you keep these concepts in mind. That way, you can better implement your plans to use persuasion as part of your schemes.

Reciprocity

Cialdini's first principle of persuasion states that human beings are programmed to return favors received and repay their debts, to treat others as they have treated us.

Individuals are obligated by nature to provide discounts or concessions to others if they have received benefits from those same people, according to the concept of reciprocity. Humans just despise feeling beholden to others, according to psychology.

This is one of the most important principles that you can keep in mind. Reciprocity consists of giving something to get something. If you expect to get something in exchange for nothing, then you might be surprised to find that that is not quite so easy.

The way reciprocity works are that you need to give something of apparent value to something of greater value, or at least what you really want to get from the other party. A good example of this is information. When you are seeking to extract information from your intended target, you may find it useful to give them some information which they might think is useful. When this occurs, the other party may be motivated to share with you the information that you want to know.

Also, reciprocity can be applied to building capital. This can come in the way of doing favors for others. So, when you build up this capital, others will then feel compelled to do what you want when you "call-in" a favor. This may seem somewhat underhanded, but it is certainly effective. That is why you shouldn't balk at helping people if you have the chance. You never know when someone else might be of service to you.

Commitment and Consistency

The principle of commitment states that humans have a deep need to be seen as consistent. Therefore, once we have made a public commitment to someone or something, we are much more likely to pursue and maintain that commitment.

From a psychological point of view, this can be explained by the fact that people have aligned their commitment with their self-image.

When you are consistent, you build up a reputation that communicates to those around you that you mean business. If you are true to your word all the time, then others will have no reason to doubt your intentions. This is where you can bend the rules to suit your needs.

By the same token, being committed to your cause is a powerful tool. When you are fully committed to your cause, your job, your company, your family, or whatever is important to you, you will find that others will respond to this attitude. As a result, they will feel compelled to do what you say, especially if you lead by example.

Social Proof

On average, when people are confused or in a situation with a lack of information, they tend to consider the behavior and choices made by a large number of people to be more valid. This rule exploits the cognitive *"Bandwagon Bias."*

It's a bit like what happens when we get out of the subway, not knowing in which direction we have to go to find the exit; we instinctively follow the flow of people, believing that they know the right path.

If I have to buy a product on the internet, I will not only choose the one with the best reviews, but I'll go for the one with the most ratings.

Cialdini defined the "social test" as people who do what they watch others do. For example, if a particular restaurant is always full of people, we are more likely to try that restaurant. If our work colleagues arrive late every day, we will be more likely to do the same.

The so-called "wisdom of the crowd" is one of the most effective methods to employ the social test. It's a case of safety in numbers!

Authority

Have you ever wondered why we tend to obey authority figures, even if they are questionable, and ask others to commit questionable acts? It's human nature!

Accessories, such as work titles (e.g., Dr.) and uniforms, instill an air of authority, making it more likely that the average person will accept what that person says. You can see this in advertisements that, for example, use doctors to support their advertising campaigns.

No doubt, being in a position of authority is a great way to exert influence on others. This is called "command." Command happens when you are put into a position in which others need to respect the investiture that you receive from a higher authority. Think about the president of a country. When a person is elected president, they have functional authority over their area of responsibility. This means that those under them have no choice but to heed orders.

The other type of authority is called "leadership." Leadership consists of people doing what you say because they want to, because they believe in you, and not because they have to. When this occurs, people rally around the leader and do their bidding. This is the most sublime expression of persuasion.

If you can develop yourself into a true leader, your intentions won't really matter. Even some of the most heinous criminals have exhibited true leadership. If you can become the type of leader that people want to follow, there is no limit to what others may be willing to do for you.

Liking

What difference does it make if you have feelings for someone? It affects your odds of being affected by that person, according to Cialdini. We've arrived at Cialdini's fifth principle: compassion. Pleasure stems from a shared interest or a more superficial interest, such as physical attractiveness.

The following is how this idea can be applied to conversions: A excellent "Who we are" page should be created by a company that wishes to enhance conversion rates.

It may appear silly, but understanding that a company's "About Us" page is a chance to inform potential purchasers about the commonalities between its employees and site visitors makes sense. Because resemblance is a significant component of like, a strong "About Us" page is essential.

It is said that it's better to be feared than to be loved. While that may be true if you are a ruthless dictator, the fact is that it doesn't hurt to be likable and charming when you need to.

In general, being likable isn't all that hard. The best starting point is being polite. Politeness can get you very far in life. This is especially true when you dislike someone. While the average person might choose to make their displeasure for an individual evident, a savvy manipulator knows that it's always a good idea to be on good terms with as many people as possible.

Also, the way you dress influences others significantly. Looking your best is a great way to break down barriers between you and those around you. While you don't need to spend a great deal of money on expensive clothes, it's always a good idea to dress in a way that highlights your best features.

Think about it this way:

If your appearance reflects aggression, the people you come into contact with will automatically get on the defensive. Naturally, this is something you want to avoid unless you are looking to intimidate others. By appearing pleasant, you can ensure that others will let their guard down, thereby affording you the chance to sneak in. There, you can make the most of your opportunity to get what you want.

Please keep in mind that the average psychopath is described as someone charming and likable. Why is that? Because they need to lure their victims by providing them a false sense of security. That is a very powerful skill if you can develop it.

Scarcity

We've reached the end of Cialdini's definitive list of persuasion principles. The idea that things are more appealing when their availability is limited is known as scarcity.

We are more inclined to buy something if we are informed that it is "the last" or that a "special deal" will soon expire.

In short, we hate to lose, and that fear is a powerful motivator to encourage us to act quickly.

People naturally feel safe and secure when there is an abundance of resources around them. When this is the case, people don't feel compelled to act right away. One of the most abundant resources is time. While we don't know exactly how much time we actually have, just the mere appearance of having lots of time can make people drag their feet.

This is why advertisers use phrases such as "this offer is available for the first ten customers" or "limited time only." These phrases are meant to elicit a panic response in potential consumers. If a person feels that they won't be able to get a good deal in time, they may feel the need to rush to get it done.

The same goes for access to yourself. If you make yourself available to those around you, they may not appreciate you as much as you would like them to. However, if you make a point of becoming unavailable to others, they will value the time you give them, especially if you provide something of value to them.

So, the last thing you want is to be "available" all the time. Make a point of literally making yourself scarce. Others will learn to appreciate the willingness you have to be there for them.

Chapter 9: Characteristics of Manipulative People

Three Ways of Becoming the Victim of a Controlling Manipulator

A manipulator to succeed must have tactics that will make it possible to use people to achieve their own ultimate objective. Although the effectiveness of a manipulator consists of several hypotheses, we will look at the three characteristics which George K. Simon, a popular author in psychology, described in his book entitled "In Sheep's Clothing: Understanding and Dealing with Manipulative People."

The manipulator will have to:

- Be able to mask their hostile behavior and intentions so that the subject does not know.

- Be able to identify their intended target or victim's weaknesses to identify what strategies are most successful in achieving their objectives.

- Have some degree of impunity ready to deal with any resistance that arises due to damaging the subject. This damage can be mental or physical.

The manipulator should rather be able to hide his thoughts from others and behave as usual. Those who are deceived often do not know this, at least not at first. The manipulator will be a good person; he will behave like a best friend and maybe support the subject in some issues. When the subject is aware of the problem, the manipulator has sufficient information to compel the subject to continue.

Secondly, the manipulator must have the ability to assess their intended victims' or their victims' vulnerabilities. This can allow them to assess the methods to use to accomplish the overall objective.

Sometimes, the manipulator can do this just by watching their subject. At the same time, sometimes, they will need some sort of interaction with the subject before the full scheme comes up.

The third prerequisite is to be ruthless to the victim. This won't be good if the manipulator puts all his tasks to work and then worries how the subject is fair in the end. It is doubtful that they would go through with this project if they were interested in the subject.

The manipulator does not care about their subject or really does not care about what it might do to the victim, as long as the overall objective is achieved, either physically or emotionally.

Signs of a Manipulative Partner

A romantic partner who is controlling reflects the principles of Covert Emotional Manipulation in a specific personal way. If someone is in a relationship and clearly their partner tries to control them, they would probably be upset with what is happening, and they are looking for a way out of this.

Most controlling partners also exercise their influence as hidden as possible. Their girlfriend or wife ends up experiencing emotional manipulation without ever knowing it. It gives the manipulator the power he or she needs without the consequences of the other person's discovery or failure.

Lying

Regardless of the end goal of the manipulator, telling lies is something they are an expert at, and they will always do so that they get what they want. There are several types of lies the manipulator can use to help them achieve their final objectives. One is that they tell absolute lies; others include the omission of some information from their subjects or parts of the facts. If the manipulator is deceptive, it is because they are aware that their lies will go further along with their agenda.

To tell somebody the truth can make them not support the manipulator, and that is totally contrary to their plans. Actually, the manipulator will say a lie to persuade a subject to do something for them, and it'll be too late to solve the problem when the subject finds out about the lie.

They can tell most of the truth with this method but will withhold certain details that are upsetting or that can delay the development they are making. Those lies can be just as risky as it becomes harder and harder to state the truth, and what the lie is.

Know When You Are the Target

When you are the target of a manipulator, you will feel fear, obligation, and guilt. What will happen is that when you are being manipulated, your mind is being forced to do something you don't really want to do. You will probably feel cared for if you do not do it, obligated to do it, and guilty for not doing it. The manipulator makes you feel fearful and could use violence, threats, and intimidation to manipulate you. The perpetrator creates a sense of guilt in his target. Nevertheless, although manipulators often play the victim, the fact is that they caused the problem. A person targeted by manipulators who frequently play the victim tries to help the manipulator to stop feeling guilty. The target of this type of manipulation also feels responsible for helping the victim to avoid her suffering by doing everything they can.

The most common concept of "gaslighting" is often used to describe manipulation, which makes people doubt themselves, their perceptions, memories, and feelings. A manipulative person can turn and make you think you've done wrong when you don't know what you have done wrong or interfere with the conversation. If you are gaslighted, you might feel a false sense of guilt or defensiveness, like you have failed entirely, or done something wrong, although, in fact, that is not the case.

When a person does a favor to you, and it is not for free, and it comes with strings attached to it, then that is manipulation. This is how you know you are the target of manipulation. The manipulator could be supportive and do many favors for other people. It can be very confusing to some because there are no red flags to this behavior.

How People Are Manipulated at Work

Manipulators sometimes lie or apologize and exaggerate or understate details, and provide details in a partial or biased way. They shout or display negative emotions to make you do what you want. They hope that your fear will lead you to obey. They tend to make critical comments or statements that ridicule you or show your shortcomings. When they send you feedbacks, they focus on the negative and try to make you feel inadequate. They feel guilty with the expectation that if you feel bad for them, you will adhere to their conditions. They "play stupid" to make you do what they want and insist on not understanding or learning how to do something. They can pretend to be an expert in something that is superior to you.

It is important to note that coercion doesn't necessarily mean that somebody is manipulative. It is possible we all put our own interests before someone else at one time or another and have used manipulative tactics to ensure that we got what we wanted.

Tips for Dealing with Manipulative People

1. Know Your Fundamental Human Rights

When dealing with someone who is emotionally manipulative, the sole guideline is to know your rights and stand up for them. You have the right to defend yourself and your rights, as long as you don't harm others in the process.

On the other side of the coin, you can forfeit these rights if you will hurt others in the process. Some of our fundamental human rights are as follows: You are entitled to be treated respectfully, you have the right to say how you believe, how you think, and what you want, you have the freedom to prioritize yourself, and lastly, you're entitled to receive what you pay for. Obviously, many people in our society do not respect these rights. In general, emotional manipulators want to strip your rights from you so that they can manipulate you and exploit you.

2. Keep Your Distance

One way to detect a manipulator is to see if that person acts differently in front of different people and in different situations. Everybody with a degree of this kind of social distinction tends to live in extreme situations, being very nice to one person and utterly rude to the other—or totally powerless at one moment and violent at the next. As already stated, causes are nuanced and deep-seated for persistent psychological manipulation. You don't have to adjust it or save it.

3. Avoid Self-Blame

Since the purpose of the manipulator is to try and use your vulnerabilities, it is understandable that you may not feel adequate or even blame yourself for not satisfying the manipulator. Avoid personalization or self-blame.

Consider your relationship with the manipulator and consider the following questions: Am I handled with real respect? Are the standards and criteria of this person appropriate for me? Is it one way or two to give in this relationship? In this relationship, do I ultimately feel better about myself? Your answers to these questions provide you with important clues as to whether you or another person has a "problem" in your relationship.

Toxic Friendships and Relationships

What does being in a toxic friendship or a relationship mean? A toxic friendship or relationship means that you are in a relationship or friendship that is unhealthy. It might be a relative, family, or even a wife. The relationship could be that of a friend. You're unable to have a consistent and productive bond with the other person, and this often leaves you questioning yourself. Some of the ways you can tell if you are in toxic relations are where emotional manipulation and guilt-tripping are involved. The relationship is often draining.

Chapter 10: Deception Tactics

Masking, camouflage, diversion, hand sleight, falsehoods, and concealment are some of the methods used in deception. Because the subject has faith in the agent, the agent will watch the subject's mind. The subject trusts what the agent says and may base their future intentions and universe shaping on what the agent has told them. A deception is a form of communication that uses omission and deception to persuade the subject's world to serve the agent's best interests.

Types of Deception

Five main types of deceit were identified by the Interpersonal Deception Theory.

1) **Lies:** This happens when the agent gives you information that is completely false. This knowledge will be conveyed to the subject, and the subject must accept it as fact. The subject is unable to recognize that fake information is being fed; if the subject recognizes that the material is incorrect, he or she will refuse to speak with the agent and will not be duped.

2) **Concealment:** This is another typical type of deception. It occurs when an agent hides or omits information that is relevant to the subject in a certain context, either intentionally or by action. The agent will not have deliberately lied to the client, but he will make certain that the crucial information is never revealed.

3) **Equivocation:** The agent makes statements that are contradictory, ambiguous, and/or conditional. This is done to make the subject perplexed and unsure of what is going on. It can also help you save

face as an agent if the subject comes back later and claims they were duped.

4) **Exaggeration:** This occurs when the agent exaggerates a fact or stretches the facts to some extent in order to change the story in the way it wants. The agent may not outright lie to the subject, but they will exaggerate the actual circumstance such that the subject submits to their demands.

5) **Avoidance:** This occurs when manipulators don't give straight answers or move the discussion into a different topic utilizing diversion tactics. In a dialog, avoidance occurs by rambling or otherwise talking endlessly in a meandering fashion. So, their ultimate game is to confuse the target, which makes them question the true version. When a manipulator changes the topic, it can be gradual and not entirely obvious.

Main Components of Deception

While determining which aspects manifest during deception can be difficult, certain characteristics are common to deceit. Unless the agent told a flat-out lie or was caught in deception, these characteristics are frequently undetectable. These are details that will be recalled if the agent employs the deception technique correctly. The three major components of deception are camouflage, masking, and simulation.

1) **Camouflage:** The first level of deception is camouflage. This is when the agent tries to keep the facts hidden from the target so that they are unaware that information is missing. When an agent tells half-truths when presenting information about anything, this tactic is frequently used. The subject will not be aware of the camouflage until the truth is exposed later. The agent is able to conceal the facts so that the target is unable to discover the deception by chance.

2) **Disguise**: Another part of the deception process is disguise. It occurs when the agent portrays himself to the subject as someone else. The agent can choose to keep things from the subject, such as their real identity, their occupation, who they were with, and what they do when they are out. This is more than just changing the outfit someone wears in a movie; the agent tries to fool their target by changing their entire personality. There are examples of how to disguise can be used in the deception process. One strategy is to disguise

themselves in encounters with the agent, sometimes as someone else, so that they are not recognized.

The agent will do this to re-engage a large number of people who dislike them, change their personality to appeal to more people, or otherwise achieve their objectives. In some cases, the agent who disguises the true nature of a proposal in the hopes of concealing any contentious consequence or reason for such a proposal is referred to as disguise.

3) *Simulation:* The third element of deception is simulation. The agent displays erroneous subject data. In the simulation, an agent can employ three key strategies.

> ***I.*** The first is imitation, in which the agent unintentionally portrays something that is similar to oneself. They might be discussing someone else's concept and claiming credit for it by pretending it was theirs.

> ***II.*** Fabrication is the second approach, in which an agent manipulates a real-world object to make it appear different. They may tell a tale and exaggerate it to make it sound better or worse than it actually is. While the core tale

may have occurred, items will be put on top of it, changing the entire storyline.

III. Finally, as a form simulation, we have a distraction. This is when the agent attempts to divert the subject's attention away from the facts, usually by baiting or presenting something more tempting than the truth. For example, if the husband is having an affair and suspects his wife is finding out, he may bring home a diamond ring to confuse her. The problem with this method is that it does not always work, and the agent must come up with a new way to perplex the subject in order to keep the process going.

How to Use Deception

Psychological research is the field that makes the most use of deception since it is required to determine the true results. People are particularly sensitive to how they appear to others and to themselves, according to the explanation, and their self-awareness can distort or interfere with the way the subject is studied when compared to completing research in regular conditions where they do not feel examined. The ruse is intended to make individuals feel more at ease so that the agent can achieve the best outcomes possible.

For example, the agent might be curious about the situations in which a student might cheat on a test. If the agent examines the student directly, the subjects are unlikely to admit to lying, and the agent will be unable to identify who is telling the truth and who is not. In this case, the agent should use a diversion to gain a better understanding of how cheating fraud works. Alternatively, the agent may indicate that the study is about how intuitive the topic is; you can even say that you can look at other people's answers before giving your own. The conclusion is included in this analysis.

Alternatively, the researcher could state that the goal of the study is to determine how insightful the subject is. It's possible that the subject will be told that they have the option of seeking solutions from others before presenting their own. At the conclusion of the deception experiment, the agent should question the subject what the genuine goal of the trial is and why the deception is essential. In addition, when the study is completed, some agencies will present a concise summary of the results for all participants.

How to Detect Deception

It is generally a good idea to learn how to recognize deception when it occurs if the individual wants to stop deception in their life and the mind games that follow. Unless the agent makes a mistake and delivers a straightforward or flat lie or contradicts something that is already true, it is difficult for the subject to realize that deceit is there.

Deception, on the other hand, can put a lot of strain on the agent's mind because they have to remember all of their previous comments on the issue in order for the story to be credible and consistent. If the agent makes a mistake, the subject will notice something is amiss. Because of the strain to maintain the past straight, the agent is more likely to reroute information to tip off the subject, either by non-verbal or spoken signs.

Deception detection, according to researchers, is a mental, dynamic, and sophisticated process that frequently differs from the message being transmitted. Deception, according to the Interpersonal Deceit Theory, is an iterative and complicated control mechanism that occurs between the agent who manipulates information to make it different from reality and the subject who then tries to determine if the message is accurate or not. After the message is received, the agent's activities must be linked to the subject's actions. During this encounter, the agent must reveal nonverbal and verbal details that will lead the subject to deception.

Chapter 11: Brainwashing

The Process of Brainwashing

The brainwashing process differs between when it is used on an individual versus when it is used on groups of people, and each distinction will be discussed in this chapter. The process begins with firstly the mental state at the time of the victim, as well as their social circumstances. These two form a somewhat basis for the process of brainwashing. The tricky part comes in where not every person can be brainwashed. The process targets a person who is trying to fill a space within him. The identification of such a person is key to the process of brainwashing. Such a person could be someone who has had a traumatic experience that has led to their existing reality shakeup. Take an example of many of the Western men who decided to take a trip to Syria and become terrorists who have done so because they lost a friend who was close to them or even a relative. When the life they have been living loses meaning, brainwashers can take advantage of this and form an idea of murder in their life. Once the perfect victim has been identified, the process of brainwashing begins. The myth has been brainwashers are psychopaths who will angrily try and brainwash their victims. The reality is that they tend to be calm and rational people who have their life together. Their victims usually do not have their life together as their brainwashers do. The first time the victim meets their brainwashers can be compared to when a homeless person meets a celebrity for the first time. The brainwasher will, first and foremost, try to create trust between the victim and themselves and also try to have a rapport with the victim. In order to do this, the brainwasher will try and create deep and superficial similarities. An example of a superficial similarity would be enjoying the same drink or food, while an example of a deep similarity would be the victim and the brainwasher having the same experience in their past. The brainwasher can effectively fake these experiences if needed. Where they shares with the brainwasher that they have lost a close friend, guess who has a similar story to tell? Yes, you guessed right, the brainwasher. This falsehood of emotional understanding is not the only initial aspect of brainwashing. The brainwasher will also share gifts with the victim and other favors, as well. The favors can be in the form of free meals, drinks, or even electronics, too. These favors and gifts create a sense of gratitude and indebtedness within the victim and will provide a smooth path in case of any resistance by the victim in the initial stages. An example of this kind is drawn from when American troops during the war are captured, and their captors would give them American-made cigarettes and would have a conversion with them using a respectful tone. This allows the victim to be susceptible to the brainwashing process.

After trying to create a rapport or connection with the victim, a utopian presentation is a next step in the process. A utopian process involves the brainwasher offering a solution to the problems the victim has shared with the brainwasher. The solution is given casually to avoid any negative responses from the victim as a result of feeling pressurized. The utopian solution takes the form of ideology or personality that the brainwasher is trying to turn his victim into. It could be terrorism, communism, or for the brainwasher's amusement of praise.

The Impact of Brainwashing

The process of brainwashing has shown that it is powerful, and anything powerful can have a lasting effect. One of the most severe side effects of brainwashing includes the loss of identity. The victim's psyche becomes detached from their old identity. The victim does things that before he would never do. It can be said that his old self does not exist anymore. The victim is left feeling as though their old self was not really like a dream. The victim is changed by the way he feels and thinks, and his behavior is also changed.

Post-traumatic stress disorder (PTSD) is another effect of those who manage to free themselves from brainwashing. The victims of brainwashing exhibit the same signs psychologically and physically as veterans of war. This shows that brainwashing can have a lasting effect like war.

An example of the long-term effect of brainwashing is where a victim was if free from the brainwashing held only later to return to it. This type of behavior is referred to as Stockholm syndrome. The victims will still in the future, praise their brainwasher and justify the ideas implanted while captive.

Some Brainwashing Tactics

Isolation

Isolation is a tactic used by brainwashers during brainwashing. Isolation means being away or kept apart from people or places. The brainwasher ensures that the victim is isolated in order to prevent any interference from other people that will make it harder for the victim to go along with the brainwashing process. The victims of brainwashers will be isolated from friends, families, and peers to ensure that they do not change their way of thinking.

Fear and Dependence

Fear is a very useful tactic and comes along away in accomplishing the brainwashing process. The brainwasher—for example, if he or she is dealing with a group of people—can use fear to ensure that there is obedience and his or her subjects remain loyal. Anything that threatens the new identity that the brainwasher is trying to achieve, the brainwasher can threaten the life or limbs of the subject.

Love Bombing

Love bombing involves the brainwasher trying to create a sense of family with the victim by bonding emotionally and sharing things with the victim. In turn, it makes it easier for the brainwasher to implant ideas in the victim's mind and create a new personality. Most people treasure family. They are the people who know you best and whom you were born into.

The process of guilty is where the brainwasher makes the victim believe that everything he does is wrong and that a victim is a bad person. Guilt creates doubt in the beliefs of the victim. The wrongs of the victim are exaggerated to cause a sense of guilt in the victim and bring the need for salvation in the victim.

Repetition

Others will start to accept a message that's a common belief in the community if it is mentioned enough times. In fact, studies have found that if only one person expresses the same opinion three times, he has a tremendous 90% chance to convert three people to the same view. The agent here will use repetition in order for the subject to believe and be convinced.

Routine Rituals

The agent here, while changing the routine of the old self of the subject and come up with a new routine for the subject to assume the new identity.

Physical Activities

The goal of the agent is to surround the subject as a means of control with an endless series of tiring activities. What distinguishes physical activities in brainwashing from sports is that the agent takes advantage of improved mood and group identity after physical activity to incorporate ideological beliefs that could be reinforced by exhaustion by repetition is another way of encouraging people's defenses to consider dubious ideas.

Steps of Brainwashing

Breaking Down of Self

The breaking down of one's self is the first step of the brainwashing process. The agent wants to break through the old identity of the subject, making them more fragile and open to the desired new identity during this process. This step is needed for the process to proceed. If the subject is still firmly in his determination and his old self, then the agent is not very successful with his efforts. Breaking this identity and making the subjects question themselves and their surroundings will help change identities more quickly in the subsequent steps. This is accomplished by several steps, such as an attack on the subject's identity, using guilt, self-betrayal, and then breaking point.

Possibility of Salvation

Once the agent has been effective in breaking down the self of the subject, the time has come to move to the next step.

In this step, the subject can only be saved if they are prepared to turn away from the former self and their beliefs and instead embrace the new one that is offered. The subject has the chance to understand what's around them, and they are assured that everything will be okay once they follow the desired path.

In this phase of the brainwashing phase, there are four steps: leniency, compulsion to confess, channeling of guilt, and release of guilt.

Rebuilding of Self

The subject has experienced several steps and emotional disturbance by this step. They are convinced that they are wrong and have to be fixed, and that their mistake creates their belief system and that it needs to be changed. They have been put through a lot designed to rob them of their old identity. After all, this has been done; the subject must learn with the guidance of the agent how to repair themselves.

This stage offers the agent the opportunity to introduce new ideas or concepts because the subject is a clean slate and very willing to learn how to feel better and be better.

Chapter 12: Mind Games in Relationships

What Are Mind Games?

The term "mind games" refers to a pattern of behavior in which an individual uses tactics to deceive, fool, manipulate and control people around them regardless of the nature of the relationship. As such, mind games are perfectly applicable to romantic, family, or business relationships.

Mind games are not necessarily considered ethical, but they are widely practiced as a means of having a power rush. The main purpose of using mind games in relationships is to get the upper hand. This means that the individual who chooses to play mind games does so with the intent of extracting as much benefit as they can from the other party or parties.

So, let's take a look at a number of ways in which mind games are played.

Playing Hard to Get

Unlike ultimatums, the "difficult to get" mind game can be confused easily with ordinary, healthy behavior. Nonetheless, certain fundamental differences demonstrate the "hard to get" role as a clear result of dark psychology. Therefore, the first move in recognizing "hard to get" tactics is to realize when it has turned into a deliberate attempt at manipulation.

Commonly, the "hard to get" tactic aims to develop a "chaser" situation in which the chaser is always running after the target. However, the chaser never really has a chance to catch the target. The main reason for this is that the target wishes to convey a sense of scarcity. If the target is readily available, the chaser may not comply with the target's wishes. That's why the manipulator becomes the target in this exercise.

Socially, if someone is perceived as "easy" in romantic relationships, they are considered to be of loose morals. By the same token, if someone is considered to be "hard to get," they may end up creating an aura of mystery and intrigue. This tends to "drive up the price" for those who wish to be with the target.

However, it should also be noted that being "hard to get" can be an expression of evasiveness, meaning that the individual who is playing this role simply wants to avoid any sort of commitment be it romantically, professionally, or personally. This tactic is only effective so long as there are others willing to chase. When no one is willing to chase, then the game is over.

Projecting

Projecting is often done unconsciously. When this occurs, a person is letting their true feelings show through the façade they may have chosen to create. It should be noted that truly authentic people don't have this problem as they may not be too concerned with concealing their true feelings.

When a manipulator is looking to consciously project, they use words, gestures, body language, and any other means of communication to get their message across in order to influence others.

Consider this situation:

A candidate walks into a job interview. Since they really want the job, they are confident and prepared. And even when the interviewer has a set of questions they wish to ask, the candidate controls the conversation. The interviewer is surprised to see the degree of confidence in the candidate. However, the candidate manipulates the conversation in order to avoid any uncomfortable questions. This tactic is commonly used to avoid facing issues head-on. Also, it can be used to implant ideas in the minds of people well before anyone actually says or does anything.

Sending Mixed Messages

Mixed messages are used to confuse people. When people are confused, it is much easier for the manipulator to trick them into doing something they may not be keen on doing.

For instance, mixed messages are common in a romantic relationship. One partner is quite loving one day but cold the next. The point of this behavior is to keep the other partner from feeling complacent in the relationship. What ends up happening though, is that the victim ends up exhausted emotionally and either breaks down or decides to leave the relationship.

In a professional setting, mixed messages can be a form of control. When employees don't know what to expect from their superiors, they may live in a state of fear. This leads them to make significant mistakes while trying to do their best. This type of confusion is great when looking to avoid any sort of unity within a group of employees.

Guilt-Tripping

Laying on a guilt trip can be quite effective when looking to break down someone's barriers. Now, this only works when the victim is actually susceptible to manipulation. This means that if you are trying to guilt-trip someone who is in a position of power, your attempts may ultimately backfire.

Therefore, guilt trips are highly effective when someone is vulnerable. Manipulators often look for vulnerabilities that they can exploit. When this occurs, they are able to make the most of the situation by making them feel inadequate as a consequence of their actions or behavior.

Withholding Affection

Affection is one of the most significant aspects of any relationship. Affection can be a physical manifestation such as hugging or kissing, not to mention sexual contact. Also, affection can be considered in terms of attention and kindness. Affection is given to those whom we are fond of and have established a certain type of affinity.

However, manipulation occurs when affection is used as a means of rewarding specific types of behavior. For example, parents will only be affectionate to their children when they comply with their wishes and orders. It should be noted that this practice is highly damaging to the psyche of the child as they grow up feeling insecure. Insecurities from childhood can be quite disastrous to adults. They may not be able to function properly in the real world.

That being said, withholding affection is nothing more than a blatant attempt at manipulation. This game is only effective so long as the victim is desperate for affection and will do whatever it takes to get it. Most of the time, though, victims are exhausted and end up leaving because of it.

Twisting the Facts

Playing mind games requires manipulating facts to suit the version of events of the manipulator. Often, reality doesn't necessarily benefit the manipulator. So, they need to take words out of context, put words in people's mouths, or flip arguments around to suit their agenda. This can be done through careful listening. Good manipulators are good listeners. They pay attention and poke as many holes as they can in counterarguments. The more that a manipulator can listen and gain insight into their counterparts, the easier it will be to twist things around.

Dismissing and Deflecting

When a manipulator isn't keen on the direction a conversation might be headed, they commonly choose to dismiss certain points or deflect attention. One of the most common ways of deflecting attention is to rant or simply talk endlessly. Poor debaters do this quite often.

Also, dismissing an argument on ideological or moral grounds is usually an effective way to get people to avoid certain points. While these techniques don't reflect an appropriate position, the real point is not to win the argument but rather to exhaust the opponent until they cannot continue defending their position. If the adversary becomes truly exasperated, they can make mistakes and thereby allow the manipulator to get the upper hand on them.

Subtle Erosion of Confidence

Manipulators all sorts of tricks to erode the confidence of their victims. Snide comments are one very common way. Also, manipulators are quick to point out mistakes and shortcomings. They are keen to make insightful remarks which are not intended to build but rather to destroy. They will also be quick to hone in on the weaknesses of their opponents. The important thing is to make sure that the person they are looking to bring down cannot feel good about themselves. They may even take it to a personal level by pointing out some sort of physical defect or bringing up past failures as much as possible.

Are Mind Games Normal in a Relationship?

The short answer is yes. Unfortunately, most people play mind games in one way or another. Needless to say, this isn't exactly conducive to healthy relationships. What ends up happening is that a relationship becomes strained as a result of the various tactics that may be employed. If they are applied consciously, then the manipulator may be keen on extracting a certain type of benefit. By the same token, if the manipulator acts unconsciously, then it's only a matter of time before the relationship suffers. So, it's always best to avoid mind games in healthy relationships.

Why Do People Play Mind Games?

To Manipulate

Mind games are used to manipulate people, especially when the manipulator feels they won't be able to persuade others by ordinary means. In the end, the tactics employed are meant to exhaust the target into compliance.

They Enjoy the Rush

Other times, manipulators feel a power rush from manipulating others. In a manner of speaking, it's a way of stroking their ego. This is very common in narcissists. They seek to control people, not necessarily because they want something from them, but because it is their nature to constantly be in control of everything around them. As a result, they get hooked on being in charge of everything.

This leads them to use any means necessary to control and manipulate others into doing what they want.

Test the Water

Some folks like to play games as a means of testing the waters. If they see that those around them are gullible and easily controllable, they will feel at ease. It also serves to determine if there are any potential challengers. In the end, the results of their tests enable manipulators to go about their usual routines. If they feel that the environment isn't suitable for their purposes, they may simply decide to seek an easier path.

How to Deal with Mind Games in Relationships

Having Strong Personal Boundaries

Personal boundaries are rules that we create to show others how to agree with us. Make sure you know how to establish your personal boundaries and say no if certain conduct is not accepted. You need to develop your self-esteem to ensure that you understand what you want to have strong personal borders.

Seek Advice from a Trusted Person

Often a close person to you can look more intelligently and rationally at issue. This is possible as it does not require emotional involvement on their part. This offers you more realistic and impartial feedback. It is important to seek a trusted person's opinion as you know they will have your best interest at heart. Moreover, you'll be confident in following their advice.

Call People Out on Their Behavior

Make sure that you tell the individual that you understand their actions. Don't try to win or even win the game with similar tactics. Just let the individual know that they are manipulative, and you will not stand for it. If you don't feel confident in facing them along, there is always the possibility of having others help you in confronting them. That way, you won't have to face the manipulator by putting yourself at risk.

Never Attempt to Change the Manipulator

Changing anyone, especially a dishonest person, is very difficult. It is likely just the attitude that they are deceptive, and contact doesn't solve this problem; there isn't much you can do about it. You will most definitely waste your time if you keep trying. So, it's usually best to steer clear of these types of people.

Move on from Such People

Once you have decided that you won't continue playing games, it's best to move on. This might mean extricating yourself from a given situation (for example, changing jobs) or simply cut ties with them. Often, this is one of the best decisions you can make for the sake of your mental health and emotional wellbeing.

Chapter 13: Toxic Relationships and Friendships, as well as how to avoid them

The perfect purpose of a manipulator is to enter into a long-term relationship with their target and to ensure that they have full control over the other individual. This is a very unhealthy relationship because only the manipulator will profit. The equivalent rate of support between the individuals who are in it will be part of a healthy partnership. But if you're in a marriage that seems like you're always the one that offers, you may be in a relationship with someone dishonest. A manipulative relationship will be hard to identify because the manipulation will be subtler than some other types of toxic relationships. Psychological manipulation may arise when one tries to create a power imbalance in the hope of taking advantage of another. Manipulation will have several methods that it can manifest. Still, the one topic that will continue to appear between all is that one individual, the manipulator, will benefit, and the other, the victim, will not and cannot be harmed. There are occasions when someone ends up in and does not even know a toxic relationship. The partnership may be quite ordinary, without the stress and complications you'll have to encounter later while coping with the manipulator. This will form part of the coercion method because it helps the manipulator to reach the target and take control of it without knowing the other individual. Naturally, the relationship will not begin with the drama or the drain on autonomy or other tactics that the manipulator will then use. When they started, the goal would see them right at the start and go the other way through. A different approach will be taken by the manipulator—one which is slower and slower.

In the beginning, love bombing and a lot of affection are not going to cause them any problems. When the goal is rooted and often in love, the manipulator begins changing strategies. It is not going to happen overnight and can continue for many weeks so that the objective is not reached before the adjustments are too late. At this stage, the aim has been so spent in and around the marriage that the issues and abuse are overlooked more than in the past.

Apparently, some unique indications indicate a manipulator in your own relationship. It is important to look for these indicators if you are uncertain whether anybody in your marriage is poisonous to you and causing you trouble or if it is a manipulator.

You are urged to leave your comfort zone in many ways. In order to ensure that interests are off track, the manipulator will do this socially, physically, and psychologically. The manipulator can, therefore, be the one with the upper hand and then be the one in charge along the way.

You're going to try to rid your confidence. If we begin having little self-confidence, we will be manipulated more easily because we are looking for ways to feel better. That's why a manipulator is so quick to ship back our trust to make us feel smaller and never great enough. The operator can take advantage of our weaknesses.

The secret treatment. That's where you take a small slight from the manipulator to make it a big deal. We will use silent treatment and disregard it to threaten the goal. All e-mails, chances of voice, texts, emails, and more are provided. The manipulator manages to keep everything under control and knows when the silent treatment is over.

The journey with remorse. Neither of us would like to feel guilty of anything, and if we experience that remorse, we'll do all we can to make that shame go away. This is something that the manipulator depends on, and he will accuse and excuse as much as he can for anything they had to do with.

You are denying and glossing on unresolved problems. Unhealthy marriages will flourish with many unresolved disputes as no contact occurs or because the manipulator will not want to settle such conflicts intentionally. That is because it will be easier and better for you if you trick yourself to feel that the conversation has started or finished than first collaborate with you to solve this problem.

We can now understand that this is not so good as to cope with a marriage. None of us would like to be caught up in this sort of relationship in which we feel caught up and, like the other individual, is always in charge of us. We would like our own lives to be governed. So, without taking full advantage of ourselves, we want to seek one friend who is able to let this happen. Though, before we go too far, there are some questions we need to ask ourselves in order to help us determine whether we agree that our spouse is a manipulator. When we have been through this guidebook, you will understand quite well whether you have a coercive friendship or not. Some of the measures you can do to defend yourself include recognizing your rights if you are involved in one of these partnerships. It is sometimes difficult to remember how to stand up for yourself when you have had such a friendship for a long time. Note that irrespective of what you have been instructed by the manipulator, you have fundamental rights to be protected. Such freedoms include the right to respect others, the right to express some of your opinions, desires, and beliefs, the right to set your own goals without being influenced by someone else, and the right to say no to others. You also have the ability to have a different opinion from another person to help ensure you are psychologically, mentally, and emotionally secure and can have your own life apart from another person if you choose.

These are the privileges that the manipulator can try in the long run to strip from you. This allows you to maintain the checks you want and ensures that you can do what you say. But the next time you're there, consider your freedoms, take a deep breath to your friend who's a manipulator, and then try. You are the only one who controls your life. Stay away. The best thing is always to keep away from a manipulative person. If this is too late, see if at least you can get a little space from you both. You simply give them another opportunity to learn about you, figure out your vulnerabilities, and find a way to get your future any time you have to get entangled with someone who is dishonest. Staying away from this person is the first and the only way to protect you from dishonest individuals. When you begin to feel an incentive to try to improve, go the other direction. Note that the manipulator tries to make you feel bad for you, and they want to help you get back in the marriage and take advantage of you again. Consider your own interest to stay away from the manipulator, and don't drop for the fuck that you want to feel bad and support them. It's not your fault, mind.

Another aspect a manipulator will do is to try to find the right ways to exploit the vulnerabilities. If the manipulator figures out the vulnerabilities, he will be able to use them to the full and use them against you. It makes it easy to feel inadequate, and often the target ends up constantly punishing yourself for the confusion that the manipulator creates. This is achieved by the manipulator deliberately. You know you will find ways to avoid guilt. And they know that they can always move the targets so that you can never meet the standards you set, no matter how hard you work and how long you work. It helps them to maintain control of their destination for as much time as possible.

Do not allow this to continue with the manipulator. We want to blame you for shortcomings and to guarantee that you always feel bad, and you stick around and seek validation from them so that you feel better. The implication is that none of this, nor anything of which the manipulator accuses you, is your responsibility. You have just been used to really feel bad, and it is done to make the company and your privileges more likely to be yielded. The manipulator will lose control over you if you know it is not your responsibility. Know why, yes. Learn how to say no. The partnership manipulator has come to rely on the fact that its goal is always to say yes to everything. They go through lots of information and strategies and make sure they do what they want and say yes. Knowing how to tell now is one of the fundamental rights we talked about earlier, but it is something we must look into it a little more and widening because it is definitely something that many of us, be it in a manipulative way or not, fail to express on a daily basis.

If we are worried about hurting someone else's feelings, and we think about how someone else's attitude can shift if we refuse to help them, saying yes to someone else can simply make us cry, and often, it takes great bravery. This happens regularly. Imagine, if you deal with a manipulator, how it takes to say no. No strong speech and knowing how to stand for this one will be a valuable skill that will help you to take some power away from and back from the manipulator. Obviously, they're not going to like that, and you're going to have to fight to stand up. If you tell 'no' without any remorse, whether or not you work with a manipulator will be the secret to a freer and healthier life in general. The target is never better than to be in a toxic relationship. It's a whole partnership that will depend on offering what the manipulator needs, and the aim would eventually lose something. The aim was, however, conditioned to think that this is the appropriate way to do things, so they won't realize they are in a toxic relationship until it's too late. The first step in resolving the problem can be discovering how to recognize when deceit, coercion, and other difficulties arise in your marriage. It takes time and a great deal of bravery, especially because the aim of that marriage has long been to develop confidence and self-esteem and get them through this difficult time. This takes time and courage. But when it does fall together, and the target realizes the connection in which they are and how to strengthen it, they can realize that without a manipulator, everything can really change in their existence.

Chapter BONUS

10 Strategies of Mass Manipulation by Media

Noam Chomsky, a famous critic, and linguist who has become one of the most prominent voices of intellectual resistance in the last decade has developed a list of the ten most prevalent and successful mind control tactics employed by governments to manipulate the public through the media. (¹)

1. The Strategy of Distraction

One of the most powerful weapons used by rulers to manipulate people is "distraction." Continuously shifting

---

(¹) Noam, Chomsky (2011) – *Media Control: The Spectacular Achievements of Propaganda*. Seven Stories Press the attention to the less important trivial news allows diverting the interest from much more vital issues as they are decided by political and economic lobbies to pass into the background.

2. The Gradual Strategy

Getting an unacceptable measure accepted is enough to introduce it gradually, little by little for consecutive years, in such a way that it is virtually imperceptible.

This is what has happened with the reduction in workers' rights. In several companies, measures or ways of working have been implemented, which have ended up making it accepted as normal that a worker has no guarantee of social protection. These changes would have caused a revolution if they had been implemented at one time.

The gradual strategy is based on the "Boiled Frog Principle," which is a metaphorical principle told by the American philosopher Noam Chomsky to describe the bad ability of human beings to adapt to unpleasant and harmful situations without reacting.

In truth, the boiled frog phenomenon dates back to research conducted by "John Hopkins University" in 1882. During an experiment, some American researchers noticed that by throwing a frog into a pot of boiling water, it inevitably jumped out to save itself. On the contrary, by putting the frog into a pot of cold water and heating the pot slowly but steadily, the frog would inevitably end up boiled.

This principle is applied daily in modern society through devious techniques of mass manipulation and conscience. These disguised techniques as "well-being" apparently are for the benefit of humanity, having such as better living, health, prolonging life, more and more products, more services, progress, technology, but where is all this taking us?

In fact, the principle of the boiled frog shows us that when a change is made slow enough to become invisible, it escapes to the consciousness and does not arouse, for most of humanity, no reaction, no opposition, no revolt.

3. Create Problems and Offer Solutions

This method is also called "Problem - Reaction - Solution." It consists of degenerating a given public situation or artificially creating a "problem" to cause a certain "reaction" from the public, with the aim of the instigator of the measures that desired to accept as a "solution" to the problem. For example: to let urban violence escalate or to organize terrorist attacks, with the objective that the citizens themselves require the government to enact new security laws at the expense of freedom.

4. The Strategy of Deferring

Another technique to encourage individuals to accept an unpopular decision is to portray it as "painful but essential" and get rapid public approval for its future implementation. It's simpler to get a future sacrifice accepted than it is to have one accepted right now.

This gives the general public more time to grow acclimated to the thought of change and, when the time comes, accept it with resignation.

5. Treat People Like Children

Many of the television messages, especially advertisers, tend to speak to the public, treating them as if they were children. They use words, arguments, gestures, and intonation as if the viewer were a child.

The goal is to overcome people's resistance. This is one of the strategies of mass manipulation that tries to neutralize people's critical sense by leveraging their suggestibility. Politicians also employ these tactics, sometimes showing themselves as father figures.

6. Taking Advantage of the Emotional Aspect

Often, the messages proposed by power aim at generating emotions and reaching the unconscious of individuals. Using emotions is a classic technique to cause a kind of "short circuit" on the rational part of the individual.

Also, the use of the emotional register allows you to open the door to the unconscious, grafting ideas, desires, fears, or inducing behavior in individuals.

7. Keep the Public Ignorant

Keeping people ignorant is one of the methods used by the power to exercise control over citizens. Ignorance means preventing people from having the tools of analysis on their own. Therefore, it means drowning out curiosity for knowledge, not increasing the quality of education, and promoting a strong discrepancy between the quality of private and public education.

8. Making the Public Complacent

Most fashions and trends brands are not created spontaneously. Almost always, they are induced and promoted from a center of power that exerts its influence to create waves of mass tastes, interests, and opinions.

The media usually promote fashions and trends brands, most of them around ephemeral, unnecessary, and even ridiculous lifestyles. They persuade people "in fashion."

9. Reinforcing Self-Blame

Another of the strategies of mass manipulation is making the individual believe that only he is guilty of his misfortune because of his insufficient intelligence or useless efforts. Thus, instead of rebelling against the system, the individual self-assesses and holds himself responsible, which in turn creates a depressive state, one of the effects of which is the inhibition of his action. And without action, there is no revolution!

10. Knowing People Better Than They Know Themselves

Over the past 60 years, rapid advances in science have generated a growing gap between the knowledge of individuals and that possessed and used by dominant lobbies. Thanks to neuroscience and applied psychology, the "system" has managed to know the individual better than he knows himself. This means that the system exercises are more in control over people than the individual himself.

Conclusion

Thank you for making it through to the end of *Dark Psychology Secrets: The Beginner's Guide to Learn Covert Emotional Manipulation, NLP, Mind Control Techniques & Brainwashing. Discover the Art of Reading People & Influence Human Behavior!*

Let's hope it was useful and gave you all the tools you need to attain your objectives, whatever they may be.

Now that you've finished this book, you should have a good idea of how to get started with dark psychology, as well as a tactic or two, or three, that you're eager to test out for the first time. However, before you go ahead and start giving it your all, you should have reasonable expectations for the degree of success you may expect in the near future.

The next step is to simply put this knowledge into practice. The great thing about this book is that it contains absolutely everything you need. The only thing you need to do next is to use it. This is an ongoing learning process for the rest of your life, so you can refer back to this book as often as you need.

While it is true that some people achieve significant success straight away, it is an unfortunate truth of life that these individuals are the exception rather than the rule. This means you can anticipate to go through a learning curve, especially when you're initially discovering out what works best for you. This is entirely natural, and if you stick with it, you'll come out on the other side stronger. Rather of getting your hopes up to an unreasonable level, consider of your time spent honing your abilities as a marathon rather than a sprint, which implies that slow and steady will always win the race.

Bibliography

Morin, C. (2019). *The Persuasion Code: How Neuromarketing Can Help You Persuade Anyone, Anywhere, Anytime.* Wiley.

Tali Sharot. (2018). *The Influential Mind: What the Brain Reveals About Our Power to Change Others.* Picador USA.

Cialdini, R. (2017). *Pre~Suasion: A Revolutionary Way to Influence and Persuade.* HarperCollins.

Cialdini, R. (1993). *Influence: The Psychology of Persuasion* (3rd ed.). HarperCollins.

Vance Packard (2007). *The Hidden Persuaders.* Ig Publishing.

A. Tversky, D. Kahneman (1974). *Judgment under Uncertainty: Heuristics and Biases.* Cambridge University Press.

J. Dantalion, (2008). *Mind Control Language Patterns.* Mind Control Publishing.

James, O. (2018). *Love bombing: Reset your child's emotional thermostat.* Routledge.

Dilts, R., (2017). *Sleight of Mouth: The Magic of Conversational Belief Change.* Dilts Strategy Group.

Bandler, R. (1992). *Magic in Action.* Meta Publications.

Brown, D. (2007). *Tricks of the Mind.* Channel 4 Books.

Christie, R., & Geis, F. L. (2013). *Studies in Machiavellianism.* Academic Press.

Taylor, K. (2006). *Brainwashing: The Science of Thought Control.* Oxford University Press.

Behary, W. (2013). *Disarming the Narcissist: Surviving & Thriving with the Self-Absorbed.* New Harbinger Publications.

Lifton, R. (1989). *Thought reform and the psychology of totalism* (2nd ed.). University of North Carolina Press

Other book by the same author

https://www.amazon.com/dp/B08R3Y6NTC

Download the Audio Book Version
of This Book for F R E E

If you love listening to audio books on-the-go, I have great news for you. You can download the audio book version of this book for F R E E just by signing up for a F R E E 30-day audible trial! See below for more details!

Audible Trial Benefits

As an audible customer, you will receive the below benefits with your 30-day free trial:

- F R E E audible book copy of this book.
- After the trial, you will get 1 credit each month to use on any audiobook;

- Your credits automatically roll over to the next month if you don't use them;
- Choose from Audible's 200,000 + titles;
- Listen anywhere with the Audible app across multiple devices;
- Make easy, no-hassle exchanges of any audiobook you don't love;
- Keep your audiobooks forever, even if you cancel your membership;
- And much more....

Click the links below

to get started!

For Audible U S

For Audible U K

For Audible F R

For Audible D E

Made in United States
Troutdale, OR
09/15/2024